LIFE WORLD LIBRARY

CENTRAL
AMERICA

TIME
LIFE
BOOKS
®

LIFE WORLD LIBRARY
LIFE NATURE LIBRARY
LIFE SCIENCE LIBRARY
THE LIFE HISTORY OF THE UNITED STATES
GREAT AGES OF MAN
TIME-LIFE LIBRARY OF ART
TIME READING PROGRAM
INTERNATIONAL BOOK SOCIETY

LIFE Pictorial Atlas of the World
The Epic of Man
The Wonders of Life on Earth
The World We Live In
The World's Great Religions
The LIFE Book of Christmas
LIFE's Picture History of Western Man
The LIFE Treasury of American Folklore
America's Arts and Skills
300 Years of American Painting
The Second World War
LIFE's Picture History of World War II
Picture Cook Book
LIFE Guide to Paris

LIFE WORLD LIBRARY

CENTRAL AMERICA

by Harold Lavine

and The Editors of LIFE

TIME INCORPORATED   NEW YORK

COVER: Dressed in traditional costume,
Indians gather in their native
village, Santiago Atitlán in the
Guatemalan highlands.

ABOUT THE WRITER

Harold Lavine, author of the interpretive text for this volume of the LIFE World
Library, is a veteran American writer, foreign correspondent and editor who has
had wide experience reporting Latin American affairs. He began his career on the
New York *American* in 1932, and subsequently worked on other New York news-
papers, including *PM,* of which he became assistant managing editor. During
World War II he served as a noncommissioned officer with the Army News Serv-
ice. After the war he joined *Newsweek* as a staff writer. He covered the Korean
War for that publication, became its national affairs editor in 1956 and chief Latin
American correspondent in 1960. In that post he reported developments through-
out Latin America, particularly in the Central American countries and in Cuba.
Now a senior editor of *Forbes* magazine, he returned to Central America in 1964
to gather fresh material for this volume.

Central America © 1964 by Time Inc. All rights reserved.
Published simultaneously in Canada.
Library of Congress catalogue card number 64-8364.
School and library distribution by Silver Burdett Company.

Contents

TR from OR - 2\83   6.60

TIME-LIFE BOOKS

EDITOR
Maitland A. Edey
TEXT DIRECTOR   ART DIRECTOR
Jerry Korn   Edward A. Hamilton
CHIEF OF RESEARCH
Beatrice T. Dobie
Assistant Text Director: Harold C. Field
Assistant Art Director: Arnold C. Holeywell
Assistant Chiefs of Research:
Monica O. Horne, Martha Turner

•

PUBLISHER
Rhett Austell
General Manager: Joseph C. Hazen Jr.
Business Manager: John D. McSweeney
Circulation Director: Joan D. Manley
Publishing Board: Nicholas Benton, Louis Bronzo,
James Wendell Forbes, John S. Wiseman

LIFE MAGAZINE

EDITOR: Edward K. Thompson
MANAGING EDITOR: George P. Hunt
PUBLISHER: Jerome S. Hardy

LIFE WORLD LIBRARY

SERIES EDITOR: Oliver E. Allen
Editorial Staff for *Central America:*
Assistant Editor: Jay Brennan
Designer: Ben Schultz
Chief Researcher: Grace Brynolson
Researchers: Jill Adams, Sondra Albert, Paula von Haimberger Arno,
Rebecca Chaitin, Irene Ertugrul, Evelyn Hauptman,
Madeleine Richards, Louise Samuels, Ruth Silva, Sigrid T. Whitman

EDITORIAL PRODUCTION
Color Director: Robert L. Young
Copy Staff: Marian Gordon Goldman, Patricia Miller,
Dolores A. Littles
Picture Bureau: Margaret K. Goldsmith, Barbara Sullivan
Art Assistants: James D. Smith, John M. Woods

The interpretive text for the chapters of this book was written by Harold Lavine and the picture essays were written by Simon Johnson and David S. Thomson. Many of the photographs were taken by Howard Sochurek. Valuable help was provided by the following individuals and departments of Time Inc.: Doris O'Neil, Chief of the LIFE Picture Library; Peter Draz, Chief of the Bureau of Editorial Reference; and Richard M. Clurman, Chief of the TIME-LIFE News Service.

Introduction

It seems apparent that the civilization which man creates cannot remain static: it either advances or retrogresses. The history of Central America amply illustrates this principle. Here, a thousand years ago, in what was the domain of the Maya, flourished a vibrant civilization which was remarkably advanced, mature and complex. Then a change occurred, the reasons for which are even today unexplained. This thriving civilization lost momentum, faltered and abruptly declined. The jungle reclaimed title to its own, and the region became lost in lethargy.

This was the land that formed the link between the two great continents of the New World, blocking Columbus in his search for Cathay. To it came Spaniards to conquer and plunder. Booty was here to be had for the taking, and the lure of it brought men not only from Spain but from many other lands. Central America became the crossroads of the world, the bridge between East and West. Here in the wake of conquest came more Europeans, Asians and Africans, establishing a potpourri of cultures which was superimposed on the remnants of the past.

As a succession of strongmen struggled for power and wealth, political and social turmoil ensued. Yet the turmoil within and the migrations from without have given a new vitality to the society in all aspects—political, social and economic.

These six countries during the past several hundred years have falteringly, though hopefully, taken "two steps forward and one step back." There were many men who had the vision of building a future that would rival the past by welding the Central American republics into a political federation.

But union has been unusually difficult to achieve under the negating influence of intense nationalism coupled with a turbulent political heritage. Indeed, there has been no historical precedent upon which to build. Even the Maya civilization was but a nebulously built confederation lacking the essentials for cohesion.

As a result, Central America's political units have remained small in area. Individually, each of the countries is characterized by a primary commitment to an agricultural economy, and each suffers from a lack of natural resources and a constricted market.

Today it is gratifying to note that the area is again generating momentum, and I am convinced that there is a renaissance in the making for these nations. There is a new and concerted movement toward an economic federation based upon the concept of a common market. Of importance, also, is the fact that the hope of political affiliation remains alive. As cooperation continues to grow, the influence of the Central American nations will be amplified, and their role in international economic and political affairs will take on great importance.

Therefore, it is urgently necessary that we try to know and understand these nations and their peoples. I find this volume to be not only interesting and authoritative but particularly useful in bringing the past, the present and the future of these lands to the attention of an interested public in a manner which is both readable and understandable. It is quite possible that not all the opinions expressed by the author, Harold Lavine, will meet with universal acceptance, but this should be for individual judgment. The book ably accomplishes its purpose: to introduce, and to stimulate the greatest possible interest in, the region.

Hence, I am pleased to commend this volume, which compresses the events of some four and a half centuries into an understandable compass.

JOSEPH S. FARLAND
former U.S. Ambassador to Panama

INDIAN VENDORS cook food for sale over charcoal fires as they wait for shoppers at the market in Antigua, Guatemala. Markets are held once or twice weekly, often on Sundays, with both buyers and sellers coming from the immediate area.

1

Nations
Escaping
the Past

THE American writer O. Henry was a romanticist with a sense of the preposterous, and in *Cabbages and Kings*, the collection of short stories he wrote with Central America as a background, he pictured the area as a musical-comedy set, thronged with characters as entertaining as they were implausible—strutting little dictators and would-be dictators more ridiculous than menacing, gentle North American grifters and gay *bandidos* laughing at death, hot-eyed *señoritas* and barefoot Indians slumbering in the shade.

In O. Henry's Central America, even the revolutions were lighthearted as well as lightheaded. The dictators huffed and puffed. The would-be dictators denounced them as tyrants and called for *libertad*. Someone tripped on a sword and someone fired a gun. Sometimes it was the dictators who ran and sometimes the would-be dictators. No matter. Life soon resumed its normal course. The grifters recalled the cruel blows that fate had dealt them; the *bandidos* made love; the *señoritas* betrayed the *bandidos;* the Indians slumbered on.

The image of Central America that O. Henry helped create still bemuses the United States. Except when a Jacobo Arbenz Guzmán comes to power in Guatemala and brings Communists into his administration or when Panamanian students storm into the Canal Zone and raise the Panamanian flag, the U.S. almost invariably thinks of Central America with amusement. When O. Henry was writing at the turn of the century, Central America, in popular American thinking, had no reason for existence but the growing of bananas; the nations of Central America were regarded as being in the pockets of U.S. banana growers and, as such, were known as "the banana republics." Even today the name persists —because the image persists.

IN O. Henry's day, as now, the image failed to reflect reality. More often than not, the amusingly preposterous dictators of whom he wrote were in actuality rapacious murderers; the gentle grifters were often on the run from the law; the *bandidos* were as gay as Murder, Incorporated; the slumbering Indians were dying of dysentery; and bananas were not as important as coffee, which has always been more vital to the Central American economy.

In fact, ever since the first Spaniards landed there, Central America has served as the stage not of a comedy but a tragedy. Its history is one of struggle: of Spaniards against Indians, Englishmen against Spaniards, U.S. Marines against Central Americans and Central Americans against one another.

One reason—the most important one—that men have fought over Central America is the same as the reason they are said to climb Mount Everest: it is there. Central America is the link between North and South America. It also provides the shortest route between the Atlantic and the Pacific Oceans. It was the route the Spaniards employed to ship the silver and gold of Peru to Spain even after French, Dutch and English pirates—men like Henry Morgan—made themselves wealthy by repeated attacks on the treasure-laden ports and fleets. Later, it was the route thousands of "forty-niners" used to get to California. Since the building of the Panama Canal, it has become one of the principal crossroads of the world.

Because Central America has been regarded merely as a bone to fight over, the Europeans and Americans rarely have dealt kindly or fairly with it. The Panamanians still have grievances against the U.S., and the memory of past grievances still rankles elsewhere. Unfortunately, too, the Central Americans themselves rarely have dealt kindly or fairly with one another. Few nations have suffered from misrule

for as many years as the Central American republics —and as a whole the area suffers from misrule still.

The region suffers, also, from the unconscionable exploitation of the poor by the rich and powerful. Except in Costa Rica, the pattern everywhere is the same: the land and the wealth are concentrated in the hands of a few, while overwhelming numbers of people live in abject poverty. And Central America suffers, finally, from one of the most vicious population explosions in the world: an average increase of 3.4 per cent a year.

Under the circumstances, it is not surprising that, as a group, the nations of Central America should be among the most backward and poverty-stricken in all of Latin America. Until he was ousted from the presidency of Honduras in 1963 by a military cabal that considered him too liberal, Dr. Ramón Villeda Morales was fond of saying that Honduras was "the country of the four seventies—seventy per cent illiteracy, seventy per cent illegitimacy, seventy per cent rural population, seventy per cent avoidable deaths." The statement is true of much of Central America, within a percentage point or two.

PERHAPS fortunately, perhaps unfortunately (since it bemuses the romanticists), backward, poverty-stricken nations often are extremely picturesque as well, and few nations are more picturesque than those of Central America. The Indians in the highlands of Guatemala still live in thatch-roofed homes of adobe, very much as their ancestors did 400 years ago; although they are Roman Catholics, they still worship gods that their ancestors paid homage to long ago; if they attend Mass, they also practice pagan rites. They farm very much as their ancestors did, planting maize with a pointed stick, and they engage in many of the same crafts. Each village has its own distinctive, brightly colored costume; the design of the costume often goes back a thousand years.

The Indians of Panama—the Cuna, Guaymí and Chocó—live even more in the past, for the Spaniards never conquered them completely; even today the Panamanian Government practices a kind of coexistence with them. Without the Indians' permission, no outsider may buy land or establish a business in their territory, nor is any outsider permitted to spend the night on the San Blas Islands that they inhabit.

In Costa Rica only a handful of Indians is left. The few who lived there when the Spaniards came either fled or died on Spanish plantations. But the descendants of the Spaniards are picturesque, too. In San José, Costa Rica's capital, the girls still gather in the central park at dusk to walk arm in arm, round and round, while the young men in the city walk in the opposite direction, appraising them.

In Granada, the first city founded by the Spaniards in Nicaragua, the inhabitants still dance *el baile de los diablitos*—"the dance of the little devils." Grotesquely dressed in brilliantly colored costumes patterned on those of colonial times —but wearing Indian headdresses—they prance from house to house, accompanied by a guitarist. Like many other institutions in Central America, "the dance of the little devils" is partly Indian, partly Spanish.

Almost everywhere in Central America, in fact, the 16th, 17th, 18th and 19th Centuries still live. But the old ways are dying. Central America is emerging into the 20th Century—more slowly, perhaps, than Central Americans impatient with backwardness and poverty might hope, but all too quickly for those who relish the picturesque. One by one the Indians are coming down from the mountains into the cities. The population explosion is driving them down, for the land can feed only so many people. Once in the cities, settled in malodorous slums, they inevitably abandon their old customs. And in the cities they learn to desire the appurtenances of the 20th Century—the television sets, the automobiles.

Factories are springing up and a middle class is developing, a class that resents the monopoly of power which those who hold the wealth still enjoy. Office buildings are rising, and girls whose mothers never left home without a chaperon are swarming to work as stenographers and secretaries. Slowly the oxcarts are giving way to pickup trucks and the handwoven costumes to machine-made cotton dresses.

The change is not taking place everywhere. If San Salvador, the capital of El Salvador, bustles like Chicago and New York, the clocks in Panchimalco, a village only a few miles from the capital, all seem to have stopped in 1529. If upper-class women in San Salvador wear clothes from New York and Paris, the women of Panchimalco still plod about in the dress their ancestors wore—a loose blouse, a long, full skirt of many colors and a shawl. Still, the change is occurring. And not only those who relish the picturesque are unhappy about it. In most of the countries of Central America, the rich and the powerful (the words are, in fact, synonymous) stand in fear and defiance of the 20th Century. For change is bringing turmoil. The middle class knows that it can rise only by destroying the system under which Central America became the private estate of a handful of families, and "the oligarchies," as these groups are called, understand that fact, too.

And both the oligarchs and the middle classes are threatened by the increasing discontent of the lower classes. Having learned to want a share of the amenities of the 20th Century, the inhabitants of the slums, who were dwelling in the 17th Century only a year or two ago, understandably are receptive to Communist propaganda.

The fact is that O. Henry's Indians never were really slumbering. They were merely silent because they realized that whoever finally won the battle— the dictator or the would-be dictator—life for them would not change. They are silent no longer.

It is easy to generalize about Central America, but it also is difficult. Central America consists of six nations united by geography, a common language and a similar history—and yet divided. They are united by geography because all six are part of the link

A GUIDE TO PROPER NAMES

Proper names in Central America are composed of three elements: Christian name, father's family name and mother's family name. For example, the family name of Dr. Guillermo Sevilla Sacasa, a Nicaraguan diplomat, is Sevilla; his mother's surname was Sacasa. It is a matter of preference whether a man uses one or both names. Carlos Castillo Armas, the late President of Guatemala, was usually referred to as "Castillo Armas," seldom solely as "Castillo." On the other hand, Anastasio Somoza García, the late President of Nicaragua, was almost invariably referred to only as "Somoza." A woman, when she marries, usually drops her mother's maiden name and adds her husband's family name, prefixed by "de." Thus Lillian Somoza Debayle, daughter of President Somoza, became Lillian Somoza de Sevilla when she married Guillermo Sevilla Sacasa.

between North and South America, a ribbon of land stretching 1,200 miles from the Mexican border to Colombia, roughly 220,000 square miles of ragged mountains, high plateaus and steaming jungles. They are also divided by geography because, until recently, the mountains, plateaus and jungles separated them from one another.

Under the Spaniards, the entire region, with the exception of Panama, had a common Government, whose capital lay in Guatemala. Panama was first a part of the Viceroyalty of Peru, and then was assigned to the Viceroyalty of New Granada, which included present-day Colombia. After the breakup of the Spanish Empire, it was a part of Colombia. In 1903 Panama broke away from Colombia with the help of the United States. Because of the United States presence in the Canal Zone, Panama's fortunes became closely linked with U.S. policies. Today, while the Canal Zone remains a basic prop of the Panamanian economy, and the country is thus closely linked economically to the United States, Panama is a politically independent Central American nation.

Quite aside from its somewhat dissimilar history, the mere fact that Panama is the narrowest part of the land bridge between North and South America made it from the very first different from the rest of Central America. Even before the building of the Canal, much of the world used Panama as a passageway. The Indians who originally inhabited Panama and the Spaniards who took it from them eventually were joined by Englishmen, Irishmen, North Americans, Chinese, Syrians, Frenchmen, Lebanese and people from a dozen other nations. The largest group to come consisted of Negroes from the West Indies, who were imported to build the railroad across the Isthmus and, after that, the Panama Canal. As a result, Panama

ISOLATED OUTPOST OF BRITISH RULE

British Honduras, an isolated remnant of British empire, perches on the northeast corner of Central America. It is small, with only 8,866 square miles of land, and poor, the chief product being mahogany. Only British funds keep the economy from collapsing. One third of the colony's 94,000 people live in tin-roofed shacks in Belize City, the capital. The first Europeans to discover and claim the area were Spanish, but the irregular coastline made it a haven for pirates, mostly British, and the first important settlement was made by British adventurers in 1638. The British jurisdiction over the area is based on a victory by British ships over a Spanish naval force in 1798. Since 1821, when Spain's Central American colonies declared their independence, neighboring Guatemala has claimed sovereignty over British Honduras, but the British insist that the area is theirs by right of conquest. The people of British Honduras do not want to be Guatemalans; they do, however, want increased self-government. Britain granted them self-rule on January 1, 1964.

is a mélange of peoples, traditions and cultures.

Panama is thus unique in Central America. However, the others also developed in different ways because of their geographic isolation. Costa Rica is basically a white nation; only 3 per cent of its population is pure Negro or Indian. Guatemala, on the other hand, can only be called Indian; more than half of the people are Indians and the rest are mestizos (mixed Indian and white). In El Salvador, only 20 per cent of the inhabitants are Indians and only 5 per cent are white; almost everyone else is a mestizo. The same is basically true of Honduras and Nicaragua, although Nicaragua also has a recognizable number of persons of Negro and white ancestry and others of Indian and Negro descent.

The nations are also different politically. Costa Rica is a democratic country. The literacy rate is high (79 per cent, as compared, for example, with Guatemala's 30 per cent); the people are so-phisticated politically; the Government almost rubs shoulders with its citizens. It is the kind of country in which an incident like this can occur: One day in 1953, when he was President, Otilio Ulate decided to walk home for lunch. On the street he was accosted by a farm worker who said, "Don Otilio, if you have a moment, I'd like to discuss my problem with you." The farm worker told Ulate that his roof was leaking. The manager of the farm on which he was employed had promised time and time again to repair it but had not done so—a violation of Costa Rica's housing-repair laws. Could the President make him do it? The President said, "Yes, of course." He took out an old envelope and wrote down the farm worker's name and the name of the farm. When he returned to his office after lunch, he called a Government official and ordered: "Take care of this." The official did.

Guatemala, on the other hand, is ruled by its Army, which does not even make a pretense of doing so democratically. The Army took over the country in March 1963 to prevent an election that everyone agreed would have resulted in the return to power of ex-President Juan José Arévalo, a leftist who once had been at least tolerant of the Communists. Arévalo had denied that he was a Communist, but the Army did not believe his denial. Guatemala nevertheless now appears to be making more progress toward reform under Army rule than it did under the constitutionally elected Government of Miguel Ydígoras Fuentes, whom the Army ousted.

For a time it appeared that the most stalwart friend of reform in El Salvador was its Army. For many years El Salvador had a Government that was democratic on paper but in reality was merely the servant of the families who own the country, the Catorce Grande, or "Big Fourteen," as they are called. This Government was ousted in October 1960 by a mildly leftist junta of Army officers and civilians. This junta, in turn, was ousted shortly after by another whose members feared rightly or wrongly that it was "soft on Communism."

THE U.S.-CONTROLLED CANAL ZONE

Cutting across the narrowest section of the Central American isthmus is what amounts to a piece of the United States—the Panama Canal Zone. The Zone was created in 1903 by a treaty signed between Panama and the United States. According to this treaty, the Zone remains Panamanian soil, but the U.S. holds in perpetuity the use of, and the right to act as sovereign within, the 10-mile-wide and 50-mile-long strip of land. The original price was $10 million and a yearly rent of $250,000. The yearly rent now stands at $1.93 million. Thirty-six thousand U.S. citizens currently live in the Zone, which has a total population of 45,000. Much of the Zone even looks like the U.S., with neat suburban-style houses, golf courses and baseball diamonds. It is administered by a governor who is appointed by the Secretary of the Army who is in turn directly responsible for Zone affairs to the U.S. President. The governor is traditionally an officer of the U.S. Army Corps of Engineers—the corps that originally planned and supervised the digging of the Canal.

Often, Army officers who oust a government because it is "soft on Communism" really do not care very much about the threat of Communism; they want power and the opportunities for wealth that power brings. This did not prove true in El Salvador. The Salvadoran Army officers, most of whom came from the lower classes, instituted many reforms. They cut rents in slum areas, for example, and established a minimum wage. They decreed that every agricultural worker should have one day off a week with pay. To the consternation of the Catorce Grande, they even nationalized the country's Central Reserve Bank, which was owned by the Catorce.

Having done this, the Army permitted elections to be held. El Salvador now has a Government that is democratic not merely on paper but in reality. Yet this apparently satisfactory state of affairs may be only transitory; many Salvadoran liberals complain that the new regime is becoming the servant of the Catorce, as were other governments before it.

In Honduras the Army ousted Ramón Villeda Morales and took over the country on the pretext that he was "soft on Communism" but really because it feared his efforts at reform. One of the leaders of the coup once told a U.S. correspondent: "Villeda Morales was a woolhead. He wanted to build schools. He wanted to build roads. He didn't realize he was opening the way to Communism."

The reporter wondered why schools and roads should lead Honduras to Communism. "Look," said the Honduran, "those Indians have been living up there in the mountains for four thousand years. You say they're leading miserable lives. I won't argue. The point is: they don't know it. You build roads, they'll come down to the capital; they'll see people wearing shoes and they'll become discontented."

In 1963 Nicaragua took a small step toward representative democracy when it elected René Schick to the presidency after 37 years of rule by the Somoza family. The Somoza brothers, Luis and Tachito, however, still run the country like a private estate, as their father, President Anastasio Somoza, did until his assassination in 1956. They are able to run it because they own a sizable proportion of everything worth owning, and because Tachito Somoza commands the National Guard, which functions as both police force and army. The Somozas are so entrenched and so sure of themselves that they can afford to permit a great deal of freedom of speech, press and assembly. For the moment at least, words do not harm them; what is more, the most vocal opposition they have comes from rival oligarchs, who cannot hope to raise a mass movement against them.

In the political sense, Panama is again unique. The country is both an oligarchy and a democracy. The economic leaders of the country and the political leaders are the same people; they are related to each other by blood or marriage. No matter whom a Panamanian votes for, the likelihood is that he will put the same families back in power.

The Panamanian oligarchy is peculiarly fortunate, for it has a scapegoat—the United States—ready at hand to blame for the country's ills. Panama has very real grievances against the U.S., which the oligarchy, with the aid of Communist propaganda, has been able to magnify enormously. The oligarchy has managed to make the U.S. the whipping boy for all of Panama's troubles, including those created by the oligarchy itself. While he was Governor of the Canal Zone a few years ago, Major General William E. Potter once remarked bitterly: "As you know, Hitler came to power and kept himself in power by blaming the Jews for all Germany's problems. We Americans, we're Panama's Jews."

Understandably, the Central American Governments live in dread of Communism and particularly of the peculiar brand of Communism preached by Fidel Castro of Cuba, which a Soviet ambassador to Havana once called "Pachanga" (the Pachanga is a wild Cuban dance). In much of Latin America, the U.S. concern about Cuban Communism is considered neurotic; in Central America, Government officials insist that the U.S. is not concerned enough.

SMALL as they are, and poor as they are, the Central American Governments are working against Castro in every way they can. Guatemala served as the base for the Cuban exiles who made the abortive landing in the Bay of Pigs on Cuba's southern shore on April 17, 1961. Since then it has often been reported that several other Central American nations have permitted would-be Cuban invaders to establish training camps on their territory.

The Central American Governments are working to destroy Castro precisely because they are small

and poor. They know perfectly well how unstable they are, how easily the Communists can recruit followers among the peasantry and in the slums. They have had experience. In the 1940s, during the administrations of President Rafael Angel Calderón Guardia and his successor, Teodoro Picado Michalski, Costa Rica came perilously close to Communism. Not only did Calderón and Picado collaborate with the Communists, they became increasingly dependent upon them. Costa Rica could well have become a Communist dictatorship had it not been for a revolution staged by José Figueres Ferrer in 1948.

GUATEMALA underwent a similar experience in 1954. It came within a hair's breadth of Communist dictatorship, again because collaboration with the Communists inevitably led President Arbenz to dependence on them. In this case it was the U.S. Central Intelligence Agency in collaboration with the State Department that prevented a Communist take-over.

The United States is well aware of the Communist threat. It not only has sought to bolster the Central American Governments with economic aid; it also maintains a school in the Canal Zone for training Central and South American soldiers in fighting guerrillas. Aside from its ideological struggle with Communism, and its belief that responsible and responsive democracy represents the best hope for mankind, the U.S. cannot afford in the geopolitical sense to allow Central America to fall into Communist hands. If the Communists were to gain control of the Isthmus, operating the Panama Canal would become increasingly difficult and eventually, perhaps, impossible. And not only must the United States continue to operate the Panama Canal, it must in the very near future build a new canal—if not in Central America itself, then in neighboring Mexico or Colombia. The time is swiftly coming when the Panama route will be unable to handle all the shipping that must use it.

The old image of Central America so long held by North Americans must thus be considered more unreal than ever. Central America is far from being a land of fantasy, and it cannot be ignored by responsible nations of the world—particularly those that lie close to it.

Market stalls cluster around the church of San Felipe in Guatemala. Built in 1918, it is modeled on the Barcelona Cathedral.

Bitter Poverty in the Midst of Natural Beauty

The six Central American countries are poor, underdeveloped and often in political upheaval, but the ugliness of social conditions is accompanied by a surpassing natural beauty. After the wet season's solid sheets of rain, even fence posts spring into bloom. Under the dry season's clear blue sky, Indians in traditional dress bargain for pottery, textiles and other goods in the village markets. In Guatemala, where most of the pictures on the following pages were taken, the background is fantastically varied.

MEDITATING VISITOR strolls in the Plaza Real *(above)* in Antigua, Guatemala's colonial capital. Abandoned after a 1773 earthquake, the city and the plaza are now partially restored.

BUSTLING URBANITES stride along the main street *(below)* of Guatemala City, the country's present capital. The street is lined with cafés, shops, and theaters showing the latest films.

TRANQUILLITY of the colonial age still pervades the interior courtyard of a Spanish-style house in Chichicastenango, Guatemala. This sleepy atmosphere is preserved in the many towns and villages throughout Central America that the early Spaniards built in hopes of luring the Indians from their scattered huts and fields so that they could be controlled more easily.

TRUDGING up a cobbled street, Indians in local dress make their way to market in Chichicastenango. Few of them reside in the village proper; they live in the surrounding hills and come to town only on fiesta and market days, much like their Maya ancestors who worked on primitive farms, traveling to the great temple cities only for religious ceremonies. Most of the Indians cling to their native customs, keeping to themselves and avoiding cities. Many speak only their local dialect and often cannot understand Indians from neighboring tribes.

18

MAYOR'S HANDYMEN, the *auxiliares,* who do everything from hauling trash to police work in Santiago Atitlán, Guatemala, wear their brightly colored tribal costumes at all times.

Village Indians take such great pride in their dress, considering it shameful to wear anything else, that the Guatemalan Army permits its Indian volunteer battalions to wear tribal clothes.

CAREFUL ARTISAN decorates the wheel of an oxcart used to haul the coffee harvest. Since the railroads have replaced the carts, the art of painting the intricate designs is slowly dying out.

SKILLED WEAVER makes a huipil, the loose blouse worn by Indian women, on a loom suspended between a tree and herself. She can adjust the tension simply by moving backward.

YOUTHFUL BUSINESSMAN hawks handmade noisemakers during a Guatemala City festival. Many of the poor make their entire living by selling handicrafts or by shining shoes.

21

HOLY WEEK ceremonies combine pageantry with observance of Roman Catholic rites

PRISONERS from the Antigua jail construct a "carpet" *(left)* of colored sawdust spread in traditional patterns of flowers, birds and geometric designs in preparation for a procession on Good Friday.

WORSHIPERS dressed in Biblical costume swing incense burners over the sawdust carpet *(opposite)* as others on the cobbled street pull a flower-decked float bearing the figure of Christ carrying the Cross.

SHEPHERDS, accompanied by Roman soldiers *(below),* proceed with the float. Although professing Christianity, many Indians also practice their old pagan religion, since many of the symbols coincide.

2

The Mystery of the Maya

THE ruins are everywhere in Guatemala, in Honduras and British Honduras, and in the Mexican provinces of the Yucatán Peninsula. They are the ruins of one of the most remarkable civilizations the world has ever seen, a civilization we know as the Maya. Great architects and engineers, remarkable artists and sculptors, and especially brilliant mathematicians and astronomers, the Maya flourished through most of the first thousand years of this era. While Rome fell and Europe passed through the Middle Ages, Maya engineers built great temples and Maya mathematicians evolved a calendar as accurate for their purposes as is ours. Then, for reasons still not clear after a century of study by archeologists and anthropologists, the Maya civilization collapsed. The jungle invaded the cities, engulfing the temples and shrines, the sculptured stones and painted walls. The Maya people are still there, industrious farmers growing maize in forest clearings; but the civilization of their ancestors is gone, the property only of the jungle—and of patient scientists who laboriously piece together from pottery shard and toppled stone what this culture must have been. The scholars' investigations are by no means complete, their conclusions in many areas by no means sure, but the very mysteries they struggle with are fascinating in themselves, and the picture they have managed to put together of Maya life makes these people certainly the most interesting of all the Indian groups who lived in pre-Columbian Central America.

Who were these people who evolved this civilization? No one knows their ultimate origin, but most experts agree that, like the Indians of the United States and Canada, whom they somewhat resemble, they immigrated to the American continent from Asia, crossing the Bering Strait and drifting southward from Alaska across the plains and into Mexico. They arrived in Central America about 10,000 B.C., give or take a millennium.

Originally they were hunters, frequently on the move in search of the herds of elephants which then roamed North America and later the deer and jaguar of the Central American forests. But then they began to learn to cultivate maize and other crops, and this knowledge allowed them to become sedentary, to build villages and develop crafts. By 2000 B.C. they were living in small farming communities, collections of round huts with roofs thatched with palm leaves. They used stones to beat the maize into a meal from which the women made cereals and breads.

IN time the people of a number of these villages developed a distinct language, and along with it a distinct way of apprehending the world, of behaving toward one another, of ordering their communal life, and of worshiping the natural forces of rain and sun and night and the earth. Slowly something distinguishable as the Maya people began to emerge from the general American Indian background. By about 500 B.C. these people, living mostly in the Guatemalan hills and forests, had started on the road toward building their surprising, complex civilization.

In many ways the Maya remained as primitive as the other Indian tribes around them, who developed less sophisticated cultures. They apparently never conceived of the plow, for example, but planted their maize by jabbing holes in the ground with a fire-hardened stick. The common farmer—the average Maya man—continued to live in a one-room hut with walls made of sticks tied together and sometimes plastered over. And their religion never outgrew blood sacrifice, even human sacrifice, although (if such a thing can be imagined) they made such sacrifices with a certain ceremonial delicacy and refinement. But in other areas their achievements were remarkable.

It is customary to divide the history of Maya civilization into three periods. The first, predictably enough, is called the Formative or Preclassic. It stretches from about 500 B.C. to approximately 300 A.D. During these eight centuries, the Maya of the Guatemalan highlands and of the Pacific Coast, and later those of the lowlands, began to build the structures which are the hallmark of their culture: stone pyramids that functioned as temples. They also began to develop their hieroglyphic writing and what was to become their specialty, mathematics.

THE fact that they built pyramids has caused a number of scholars, especially those of the 19th Century, to speculate that the Maya may have come not from the heartland of Asia, but from Egypt, or at least from the Middle East. An Englishman, Lord Kingsborough, became so obsessed by the idea that the Maya were descendants of the Ten Lost Tribes of Israel that he devoted his life and fortune to trying to prove it. He wrote nine massive, illustrated volumes to this effect, paying the publishing costs himself. (The nine-volume set cost the equivalent of $3,500; few were sold.) His fortune gave out before his life, and he ended his days a bankrupt in a Dickensian debtors' prison. Some color has been lent these theories in this century by the late Harvard anthropologist Earnest Hooton, who theorized, from examining living Maya and inspecting sculptured representations of long-dead ones, that they might have come initially from the Iranian plateau and have picked up their Mongoloid characteristics during a long trek across Asia. That they built pyramids, however, seems to have had nothing to do with Egypt—it is simply an unconnected but parallel development.

As hard as it was for Lord Kingsborough and others to believe that the Maya could have created their civilization in the isolation of Central America, cut off from contact with other great cultures, that is apparently what they did. Or rather they synthesized and elaborated the skills and beliefs that were common to a number of Indian groups.

The Classic period of Maya civilization lasted from about 300 to 900 A.D. It was during this time that the Maya erected their highest and handsomest temples and built their largest and most ornate cities—Tikal, Uaxactún, Copán, Piedras Negras, Yaxchilán and others. They also erected more and more stelae —large, cut slabs of stone—in the courtyards of their temples and carved upon them beautiful bas-reliefs. The period also saw the flowering of their remarkably advanced mathematics and astronomy.

The driving force behind all this building, carving, ciphering and stargazing was religion. It was a religion which, as it developed, became extraordinarily complex, but at its center was one simple thing: maize, the Maya staff of life. If the maize grew, everyone ate; if it did not, everyone starved. But the maize crop depended, of course, on sun and rain, and so there were, the Maya conceived, not only gods of maize and the earth, but also gods of the sun, of rain and winds, and of every other natural thing that could affect their crops. They also believed that the earth had four corners, north, south, east and west, and therefore the rain god was both four and one—being himself and also four gods, one for each direction, at the same time. Prominent mountains, springs and rivers all had gods associated with them, and there were, it appears, 13 sky gods and nine gods of the underworld. Many of the gods, in addition, could and did change their sexes and ages and could be, at various times, both beneficent and malign.

BUT this was by no means all. How, the Maya wondered, could one predict the behavior of the sun god, the rain god and the other deities? Ceremonies in their honor, however fervently and carefully done, did not always produce good weather for crops. The answer, the Maya came to believe, lay in the stars and in cycles of time, and in the favorable, or unfavorable, conjunction of numbers in their calendar. Believing that the weather came in cycles, and believing that numbers had mystical importance (the numbers themselves became gods), the Maya might have wanted to know, for example (and this is simplifying a very complicated matter), when the equinox last fell on the 11th day of a month and what the weather had been like during that spring. For with such a portent, it was sure to be the same again. It was to answer such questions as this that the Maya developed their mathematics, from which in turn (aided by astronomical observation) they developed their accurate calendar. It was also the way their religion developed, for to them mathematics was a

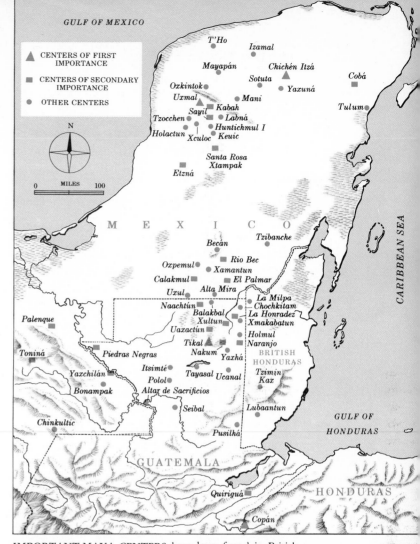

IMPORTANT MAYA CENTERS have been found in British Honduras, Honduras and Guatemala, and on the Yucatán Peninsula in eastern Mexico. The centers in Guatemala and other Central American countries were occupied mainly from 300 to 900 A.D., while most of those in Mexico flourished later, some lasting until the Spanish conquest in the 16th Century.

religion, or to turn the proposition around, their religion and its observances came to be based on mathematics. Not only numbers became gods, so did the stars, the days of the week, the months, the years.

This complex intellectual construction also determined the shape of Maya society and the shape and function of Maya cities and their architecture. To work out the mathematics, to pass its mysteries on from generation to generation, and to pass on also the knowledge of the ceremonies that were appropriate at each season of the year, there had to be a large and privileged priestly class. And that is exactly, scholars believe, what the Maya had. Their rulers, for the most part, were priests, and the priests formed the Maya aristocracy. It seems likely that each city was governed by a council headed by a *halach uinic,* who was both head priest and governor. He, like other Maya priest-aristocrats, wore resplendent clothes and jewelry—beautifully carved necklaces, anklets and bracelets of jade. They even had jade ornaments inlaid in their teeth. For ceremonial occasions they wore enormous headdresses made of the brilliantly colored feathers of jungle birds.

Some students of the Maya believe that Maya cities were not, in the modern sense, cities at all. They were primarily collections of pyramid-temples with buildings nearby whose rooms were probably not lived in but were used for small and possibly secret religious ceremonies. There may have been dwellings for the priest-aristocrats, but there were probably few inhabited by the common people. The cities, then, were not for habitation or even business (although considerable trading and commerce may have taken place in their squares), but focuses for the religious life of all the surrounding villages, where the common people, the farmers and artisans, did live.

It was these common people, of course, who provided the labor to build the great templed cities. There is no reason, though, to see them as sweated slaves of the priests, coerced with the lash. The temples were for the praise of the gods, the very gods who made the maize and the other crops grow. It was for everyone's well-being that a new and more nobly impressive pyramid should be built as the scene for next year's ceremonies.

THE pyramids are much alike in the various cities that the archeologists have discovered. They are tall—the tallest, found at Tikal, is 229 feet high—and far narrower than the Egyptian variety. They are commonly made of limestone, since that kind of stone was available near most of the building sites. They have steps all the way to their tops, for many of the most important religious ceremonies were performed by the priests in small temples on the pyramids' summits. They were almost always constructed in groups. Two would face each other, a hundred or more yards apart, with a plaza in between, where other religious ceremonies were held. Or there would be what the archeologists, borrowing the word from the Greeks, call an "acropolis"—a raised, paved platform on top of which stood a number of temples.

A curious feature common to many Maya cities is that new temples were built on top of older temples, or the older structures were clothed in new facings of limestone. This peculiarity has been of enormous aid to the archeologists who have been unearthing the remnants of Tikal and the other great Maya centers, for by digging through the various layers of construction, they have penetrated farther and farther into the Maya past. Each level downward represents a movement of a century, or two or three centuries, toward the dim beginnings of Maya culture.

ESPECIALLY helpful are the tombs. The Maya, it would seem, buried their notables in tombs beneath their pyramids. Not only have these graves, protected from the weather by levels of masonry, rendered up priceless examples of Maya jewelry and pottery (like many other peoples, the Maya provided the dead with the utensils they would need in the next world), but the entrances to the tombs, when a new temple was to be built on top, were commonly filled in with all sorts of rubbish—broken pots, old stelae and the like—in which the archeologists have found priceless clues to the Maya way of life.

Some of the other buildings in the cities may have been used by the priests as robing rooms, where they put on their gorgeous vestments and feathered headdresses. And in the cities, there is often, curiously enough, a ball court. The Maya had rubber from which they made balls, and they evidently played a game with them inside a court walled on two sides to form a playing alley. Whether the ball game was part of their religion, or a formal entertainment for the priests or just a means of relaxation from religion, we do not know.

And everywhere, there were the stelae. In Tikal, in Guatemala, the greatest of the Maya cities, more than 115 have so far been discovered. Great slabs of limestone, they stood before the pyramids and the platforms like huge sentinels. Many were carved with figures of the Maya gods and with hieroglyphs telling when they were erected and why. Some of the glyphs give information about the ruling priestly families. Others often show mathematical computations.

How the Maya built these cities and erected all these stelae (one of which, found at Quiriguá, weighs 65 tons) staggers the imagination. The workers had to quarry, shape and sculpture the stone with stone tools. They apparently did not use the wheel, and even if they had, it would have done them little good since they had no draft animals. As a result they had to carry the blocks of stone from quarry to building site, or drag them with aid of rollers, and then lift the blocks into place. But build they did for hundreds of years, raising the pyramid-temples higher and higher, erecting new temples and new stelae. After a while, the land of the Maya, which eventually was to encompass 125,000 square miles in Central America and Mexico, became a conglomeration of cities with their surrounding farm villages. Yet the Maya never joined together to form an empire. They seem to have preferred to remain in their city-states, united only by a common language, religion and culture, and by trade.

Archeologists have over the last century slowly pieced together a knowledge of how to read some of the Maya hieroglyphs. They have been aided by the three surviving Maya manuscripts—scrolls several yards long written on a kind of paper made from tree bark—which are named for the city libraries that own them: Codex Madrid, Codex Dresden and Codex Paris. Predictably, these texts are largely filled with divinatory almanacs telling which days were favorable for hunting or for sowing crops. With these, and with continued study of stelae carvings, we now can identify the stylized Maya glyphs for a number of their gods and can follow with considerable accuracy their astronomical and mathematical calculations.

MAYA math and its connection with astronomy, and the connection of both with the gods and religious observances, are far too complicated to be dealt with adequately in short compass. However, even a brief summary of a few of the Maya's achievements will give an idea of their remarkable intellectual powers.

First of all they developed a workable system of mathematical notation. Their numbers were mostly simple arrangements of dots and bars, but more importantly, they could be arranged in series, like our Arabic numerals, and could thus be added and subtracted. It is hard to add Roman numerals: one cannot just place MCDXVII above CMXXIV and add the columns—as one can with, say, 1,417 and

924. The Maya symbols could be arranged in columns and just added. To make such a system workable, of course, one needs a common factor, and the Maya had this, too. The Arabic factor we employ is 10; the Maya used the almost as convenient 20.

It is also often said that the Maya developed the concept of the zero. In a way they did, and used it in their computations, but they thought of it not as zero—nothing—but as completion and as the equivalent of 20, which, since their months had 20 days, they also thought of as completion.

THE Maya calendar, while very complicated in its details, is simple in essence. It consisted of a "vague year" of 365 days made up of 18 months of 20 days each, plus five extra days. Twenty times 18 equals 360, plus five equals 365. Some scholars believe the Maya had a mechanism for calculating what we call leap year. This "vague year" was coordinated with a "sacred year" of 260 days with which they calculated their "sacred cycle" of 52 years. What is staggering is the amount of celestial and solar observation required to arrive at such accurate measurements of time. Each astronomer's observations had to be noted with great care, compared with other observations and the data passed on from generation to generation. This was, it seems certain, one of the functions of the stelae, many of which do carry data on the path of the moon. In addition to this, the Maya astronomer-priests could accurately predict eclipses and the visitations of Venus—both highly significant in the priestly prophecies—although they could not tell whether the eclipses would be visible from Central America. Since one astronomer in a lifetime might be able to see only a half a dozen eclipses (especially considering the often cloudy weather), the mathematical computations involved in predicting them had to be both complex and accurate.

The glyphs themselves and the other carvings that appear on the stelae are very beautiful, at least to an eye accustomed to the conventions of Maya art. Everything in Maya carving is foreshortened and depth or distance only rarely indicated. The heads of the carved figures, especially those of priests adorned with their gigantic headdresses, are almost as big as the bodies to which they are attached. Snakes often writhe betwixt and about the bodies, complicating the already complex designs. But the intensity and the balance of the designs, the modeling of the gods' faces, and the expressiveness of the serpents' malevolent and rapt gazes are all striking and communicate the sort of awe all great art inspires in the beholder, regardless of subject matter or the seeming oddity of the artists' conventions.

Some of the archeologists who have devoted much of their lives to unearthing the remains of Maya civilization have claimed that it was as great as the civilizations of Greece or Rome. Their enthusiasm for, and dedication to, their field makes this exaggeration understandable, but of course such a claim *is* an exaggeration. A Maya pyramid, however grand, is not the Parthenon, and it seems very doubtful, with their concentration on religion, architecture and mathematics, that the Maya ever developed a Plato or an Aristotle, a Vergil or an Ovid. But a great and even astonishing civilization it was, nonetheless, and all the more so in its extreme isolation.

FOR reasons we can only surmise, Maya civilization came to a virtual end in the centuries before the Spaniards arrived. At Copán, the Maya appear to have ceased carving and erecting stelae in 800 A.D.; at Quiriguá, Piedras Negras and Etzná in 810; at Tila in 830; at Nakum in 849; at Tikal and Seibal in 869. These are the last dates on the stelae found in those cities. By 900 the priesthood seems to have lost its power throughout the heartland of the Maya. Little by little, the cities were abandoned. And soon the great temples were devoured by the jungle.

Scholars have developed a dozen theories about why the Maya stopped building and why they deserted the cities. There is no conclusive evidence that the Maya civilization was destroyed by war—or by a plague or pestilence, for that matter. It was long a popular theory that the Maya were forced to move because they had worn out the land they farmed, but modern agronomists say that this, too, is unlikely. A theory widely accepted today is that, in city after city, the people revolted against the priests and slaughtered them. Perhaps this was because, as Maya civilization flowered, the religion became too sophisticated for the people, who, unable any longer to understand the priests, wearied of building the pyramid-temples.

To understand the aftermath of the collapse of Classic Maya civilization, the "Postclassic Era," one must look north to Mexico. There, in about 900 A.D., a tribe called the Toltecs emerged and built an impressive capital, Tula, north of present-day Mexico City. At the end of the 10th Century, apparently, a group of these Toltecs, or a group of Indian warriors influenced by Toltec civilization, entered Yucatán. They were led by a man called Kukulcán, who was, so legend has it, Quetzalcoatl, the Mexican god of learning, whose form is that of a feathered serpent. Kukulcán's band came upon a city that had long been an important Maya cultural center, took it over and renamed it Chichén Itzá. Using this new capital as their base, the Toltecs (now called the Itzá) extended their control to other Maya centers.

But just as the Chinese absorbed successive waves of invaders, the Maya absorbed the Itzá. Soon a new civilization began to flower, a combination of the Maya and the Toltec. Old cities and old temples were rebuilt and refurbished. Sculpture appeared which utilized motifs drawn from Toltec religion—plumed serpents, prowling jaguars and eagles with unfurled wings. Yucatán eventually came to be dominated by this new Maya civilization, whose most important center was the city of Mayapán. This renaissance came to an end with the brutal revolution in Mayapán in the 15th Century.

THIS was the end of Maya civilization, but it was not the end of the Maya. For their descendants survive in Mexico and in Central America and especially in Guatemala. The Maya language survives and much of Maya religion does, too. It has been fused with Catholicism in a strange amalgam. At Chichicastenango in Guatemala, during Holy Week the descendants of the Maya burn incense on the steps of the Church of Santo Tomás in honor of the Maya gods before they enter to kneel in front of the crucifix. Inside, there are candles and the hum of prayers, but to whom the worshipers pray, to Christ or to Chac, the Maya rain god, no one can say. The worshipers themselves would be unable to answer, for in their imaginations the mysterious religion of their Spanish conquerors has long since fused completely with beliefs which were evolved long before the coming of the white man.

Lifting an incense burner from a pit at Tikal, archeologists from the University of Pennsylvania Museum excavate a Maya grave.

Digging into the Enigma of a Great Civilization

The Maya in northern Central America developed an accurate calendar, made great advances in astronomy and mathematics, built huge temple cities and left myriads of hieroglyphic carvings, but knowledge of these achievements has often led scholars to mystery. Why did the Maya construct building after building in almost frenzied succession? Were the groups of Maya buildings true cities or only ceremonial centers? What relationship did the Maya have with neighboring cultures of which present-day scholars know even less? Today, archeologists endure soggy heat, scorpions and lethal snakes as they search for the secrets of the Maya's growth and their mysterious decline long before the coming of the Spaniards.

MAGNIFICENT TEMPLE at Tikal
reveals the Maya's glory as workmen clear the overgrowth of centuries

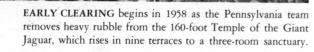

EARLY CLEARING begins in 1958 as the Pennsylvania team removes heavy rubble from the 160-foot Temple of the Giant Jaguar, which rises in nine terraces to a three-room sanctuary.

SECONDARY STAGE of the work exposes the stairway and masonry. Investigators tunneled into the 1,300-year-old temple in 1959 and found that it was built over a temple centuries older.

RESTORED STRUCTURE stands at the edge of what was once Tikal's Grand Plaza. Like many of the nearly 3,000 buildings in Tikal, the temple was made of limestone blocks, originally coated with white plaster. Rows of stelae *(foreground)* remain in their original positions in the plaza. Here the Maya held their religious ceremonies, which included elaborate processions.

CENTER for the study of astronomy, Copán was abandoned centuries ago

STONE GOD guards the steps of a temple (*right*) at Copán, Honduras, a city great in the arts as well as in science. Everything from days of the month to numbers was a god in the thinking of the Maya, and out of their preoccupation with the divinity of time and numbers arose amazingly accurate calculations of astronomical events.

TEMPLE DOORWAY is topped by a lintel, or crossbeam supporting the heavy blocks above. Skilled as they were at such elementary construction methods, the Maya builders never employed the true arch. They used the corbel, or false arch, made by inclining two walls toward each other and capping them with flat stones.

CENTRAL CORE of Copán, part of which is shown below, covers more than 75 acres, making the city one of the largest of the Classic period (300-900 A.D.). To the right are the remains of an enormous acropolis, its stairway *(right center)* carved with 2,500 undeciphered hieroglyphs, the longest single Maya inscription yet found.

EXQUISITE MINIATURES carved with rudimentary tools reveal the skills of the Maya and their neighbors

MOSAIC MASK from Tikal, only one and a half inches tall, is made of jade and shell on a stucco base that originally had a wooden core. It is from the early Classic period, 300 to 600 A.D.

GOLD FIGURINE from Williamsburg, Costa Rica, is a pendant one and one-quarter inches high. Its face shows Colombian influences, while the spread hands resemble Peruvian carvings.

FEARSOME HEADS discovered in Tikal were made of pottery around 200 B.C. by Maya of the pre-Classic period. They prefigure the flowering of later Maya achievements in the arts.

JADE BAT, two and a half inches wide, is from Costa Rica, but is difficult to date because most Costa Rican artifacts are found in shallow graves, not in well-stratified layers of earth.

PARROT DEMON incised on a polished bone was found in the Temple of the Giant Jaguar at Tikal. It is part of a larger scene carved on the bone which shows deities in a dugout canoe.

STARING STATUE, of polychrome clay, stands 12 inches high. It was found in Costa Rica but may be of Mexican origin. Scholars believe the ornamentation on it represents tattooing.

NEW FINDS from silent cities may shed light on the Maya's little-understood rise and mysterious decline

REMAINS of a high priest of Tikal *(opposite)* were discovered in the Temple of the Giant Jaguar. His body is festooned with some 200 pieces of jade—necklace, headdress, ear ornaments, bracelets and anklets. Near him lie bowls and oyster shells. Scholars believe he was buried just before the temple was built in 700 A.D., some 200 years before the collapse of Tikal.

TEMPLES of Mixco Viejo *(right)* lie in the highlands not far from Guatemala City. Unlike the Classic lowland sites, most of the highland centers do not have dated stelae, hieroglyphics or corbeled arches, and the limestone buildings are lower and less elaborate than the lowland temples. A post-Classic center, Mixco Viejo was still occupied when the Spaniards came.

Testament to the former might of Spain, the fort at San Felipe de Lara stands watch on the shore of Lake Izabal in Guatemala, where

it was built in 1652 to protect goods awaiting shipment to Spain.

3

The Spanish Conquest

THE Spaniards came for gold. They came buckled in armor, steel blade in mailed fist, ready to kill for gold or (should God so will it) be killed. Still clad in armor in spite of the scorching tropical sun, they struggled through swamps and jungles and climbed mountains in pursuit of the metal that would make them rich. For gold they did battle with Indians who outnumbered them by odds of vastly more than 100 to 1. And for gold they slaughtered each other.

To the Indians, they were madmen, to be regarded not only with hatred but with loathing. In Panama in 1514, the Indians captured several adventurers attached to the command of Pedro Arias de Avila. Arias' lust for gold and his ruthlessness with the Indians were monstrous even to his fellow Spaniards; they called him "Pedrarias the Cruel." The Indians poured molten gold down the captives' throats, crying as they did so: "Eat! Eat gold, Christians! Take your fill of gold!"

It has been said that man cannot worship both God and the Golden Calf. The Spaniards did. They were

THE CONQUEST of Central America begins when Rodrigo de Bastidas sights the Panamanian coast in 1502 (1). Columbus in 1502 claims Honduras for Spain (2), then trades with Panama's Indians (3). Balboa discovers the Pacific in 1513 (4) while Pedrarias the Cruel persecutes the Indians for gold (5). Niño and Gonzáles in 1522 set out from Panama (6); later Niño probes the Nicaraguan coast (7) and Gonzáles discovers Lake Nicaragua (8). In 1524 Alvarado kills the Indian King Tecum-Uman to subdue Guatemala (9), founds his capital, Santiago de los Caballeros (10), and takes El Salvador, establishing a fort at San Salvador (11). In 1524 Cortés sets out from Mexico (12) to wrest control of Honduras from a disloyal lieutenant,

not hypocrites; they were simply religious fanatics who hated paganism as much as they loved gold. They converted the Indians to Christianity even as they murdered them.

The first of the conquistadors to arrive in Central America was, of all things, a notary public. Perhaps for that reason Rodrigo de Bastidas was hardly typical of the conquistadors who came to Central America after him. He refused to allow his men to rob the Indians, and while he was attempting in 1525 to establish a colony in Colombia after exploring the Central American coast, they assassinated him.

In 1502, on his fourth and last voyage, Columbus himself had reached Central America. Once again he was attempting to find his way to the fabled lands of the East—Cathay, Cipango and the Indies. This time he found his path blocked by Honduras. After landing at what is now the city of Trujillo, he headed southward, down the coasts of Nicaragua and Costa Rica, still in pursuit of the westward passage. He explored the Panamanian coast nearly all the way to Colombia and at last, in despair, returned to Spain. It was not only his last voyage; it was also his most tragic. Columbus was to die only two years later, never knowing that Panama was the route to the East that he had sought, that across Panama lay the Pacific Ocean.

The names of those who followed him over the next 20 years ring through Central American history: Alonso de Ojeda, Diego de Nicuesa, Martín Fernández de Enciso, Pedro de Alvarado, Vasco Núñez de Balboa, Francisco Pizarro. The greatest of them all were Balboa and Pizarro. Balboa was to discover the Pacific, although, ironically, the English poet John Keats would give the credit to "stout Cortez" in his famous sonnet. Pizarro was to find Peru and the gold of the Inca. Their two discoveries were to make Panama the crossroads of Spanish America and bring to Spain the wealth that made it a dominant world power until the end of the 16th Century.

Olid, but Olid is killed by Cortés' followers (13). Córdoba in 1524 founds the city of Granada (14) as other Spaniards dispute possession of today's Nicaragua (15). As Spanish control solidifies, gold transportation routes are opened (16) and missionaries convert Indians to Christianity (17), but English and French pirates start attacking Spain's gold-bearing ships (18).

Spanish galleons for years unloaded Inca gold and silver at the town of Panama on the Pacific; slaves and mules carried the treasure across the Isthmus to ports on the Atlantic, where it was put aboard galleons bound for Spain.

The treachery-ridden story of the struggle for Central America actually begins in 1509, when King Ferdinand of Spain divided the territory between two of his cavaliers, giving Diego de Nicuesa the land west of the Gulf of Urabá in what is present-day Colombia and Alonso de Ojeda the land to the east. Ojeda landed in Colombia, near what is now Cartagena, hoping to establish a base for conquest. The Caribs who lived there met him with a rain of poisoned arrows. Seventy men were killed instantly. Ojeda and the remnants of his 300-man force managed to fight their way back to his ships.

Sailing westward, Ojeda encountered Nicuesa's expedition. The two men joined forces, making raids on coastal villages. Then Ojeda settled down on the shore of the Gulf of Urabá, where he founded a colony, San Sebastián. Farther west, Nicuesa built a small fort, which he named Nombre de Dios.

Ojeda fell ill, and without supplies he and his men were soon starving. Leaving his lieutenant Pizarro in charge of San Sebastián, he sailed for Hispaniola, the seat of government and supply base for the Spanish Indies, with the intention of obtaining immediate aid from his partner and friend Enciso. He arrived to find that Enciso already had sailed for Central America. Sidetracked to other adventures, Ojeda never returned to the domains he had been granted and eventually died destitute in Hispaniola.

At San Sebastián, Pizarro came to the realization that Ojeda would never return. With his men, he sailed east and came upon Enciso's expedition. Aboard Enciso's ship was Balboa, who had stowed away on the expedition to escape creditors in Hispaniola. At Balboa's suggestion Pizarro and Enciso founded the colony of Santa María de la Antigua del Darién in present-day Colombia, whose coast Balboa had visited.

PIZARRO was not yet a dominant figure. Enciso, a lawyer by profession, ran the colony with a heavy legal hand. Issuing decree after decree, he regulated virtually every minute of his men's lives. When grumbling began, Balboa turned legal weapons on the lawyer in an effort to make himself ruler of the colony. He called the men together and declared that Enciso had no right to issue decrees because Antigua was on land granted to Nicuesa. The men agreed, and Enciso was shipped off to Spain.

Soon after, a supply ship sent out from Spain reached Nicuesa at Nombre de Dios. Of his original force of 700 men, 640 were dead; only 60 starving wretches had managed to survive—on a diet of roots and shellfish. Balboa, who had got rid of Enciso by citing the fact that Nicuesa was the legal ruler of the region, now packed Nicuesa himself off to Spain. There is some question about Balboa's motives. Some accounts assert that he was attempting to aid Nicuesa. Nevertheless, the ship in which he sent Nicuesa was leaking at every seam, and it never even reached Hispaniola.

Treacherous he might have been, but Balboa also was a great soldier and a resourceful administrator. He subdued the Indians around him by setting tribe against tribe, and gradually turned Antigua into a self-supporting settlement. It was, however, an Indian named Panciaco, the son of a local chieftain, who set Balboa on the path to glory. One day, watching the Spaniards wrangling over the gold they had managed to collect, Panciaco is reported to have said: "Cease your unseemly brawl and I will show you a country where you may obtain your fill of gold. Beyond these hills is a sea and beyond that sea is a king whose people eat from plates of gold."

BALBOA'S desire to find the sea and the land Panciaco talked about was inflamed by news from Spain. Enciso had reached Madrid and accused Balboa of treachery. With powerful friends at court, Enciso was determined to revenge himself on Balboa. Realizing that his best chance of gaining the favor of the King lay in finding gold for the royal treasury, Balboa gathered together a force of 190 Spaniards and 1,000 Indian slaves and allies and sailed in the direction Panciaco had indicated.

With directions from his Indian advisers, Balboa was able to drop anchor at a place on the coast of Panama where the Isthmus is relatively narrow. The exact point of his anchorage is not known; it lies somewhere near Punta Sasardí. Leaving a party behind to look after his ships, he plunged into a jungle so dense that even at noon the sun could not penetrate it. His men had to hack their way with their swords and climb the Central American mountain range known as the Cordillera de San Blas. Everywhere, there were Indians to fight.

Twenty days after entering the jungle, Balboa and 66 of his men reached the foot of a hill. A breeze stirred. It was cool and it smelled of salt. Alone, Balboa climbed the hill on September 25, 1513, and there, in Keats's words, "silent upon a peak in Darien" he became the first European to look on the eastern shores of the Pacific.

Balboa's triumph was not to last. Enciso kept up his vendetta at the Spanish court. In part because of his efforts, Pedro Arias de Avila was appointed Governor of Darién. Jealous of Balboa's exploits and popularity (Balboa had been given the title of *Adelantado,* or King's Deputy, after news of the discovery of the Pacific had reached Spain), Pedrarias ordered Pizarro, Balboa's lieutenant, to arrest him.

Charged with treason, Balboa was found guilty and was beheaded in 1519.

In the cold light of retrospect, the Spanish battle for Central America was almost senseless. The Indians did have gold—but very little, hardly enough to be worth suffering and dying for. The real gold lay in the land Panciaco had told Balboa about, Peru, which Pizarro was not to conquer until the 1530s.

The Spaniards of course had no way of knowing that at the time. Central America seemed a rich prize, and there were plenty of men willing to fight for it. Gil Gonzáles Dávila came from Hispaniola to carve a Central American empire for himself and succeeded in making at least a start on one. Hernán Cortés, the conqueror of Mexico, sent a lieutenant, Cristóbal de Olid, to seize Honduras. Olid decided to double-cross Cortés and take Honduras for himself. Outraged, Cortés sent another lieutenant, Francisco de Las Casas, to capture Olid. Olid instead captured Las Casas and also made a prisoner of Gil Gonzáles Dávila. Olid then made the fatal mistake of spending an evening in the company of his prisoners; they killed him and turned his conquests over to Cortés.

Cortés sent still another officer, Pedro de Alvarado, to explore and conquer Guatemala, and it was Alvarado who finally brought peace to Central America—peace by the sword. A tall, handsome man with a reddish beard, he was called *Tonatiun,* "the Sun," by the Indians. He was impulsive, often rash, and fearless. His opponents were no less so. During the Guatemalan campaign, he wrote Cortés: ". . . we are in the hardiest land of people that has been seen; and so that the Lord may give us victory, I appeal to your Grace to order services . . . by all the clerics and friars, to ask Our Lady's intercession; for we are far removed from succor unless it is to reach us from there."

EVENTUALLY, Alvarado subdued much of Central America, and only three decades after Columbus' landfall, Spain stood supreme in the region. Alvarado extended his sway from Guatemala to El Salvador and in 1539 took over Honduras. As Captain-General, the chief military and civil official of the area, he founded Santiago de los Caballeros, the first capital of Guatemala, and San Salvador, the present capital of El Salvador.

In 1540 Alvarado attempted to crown his successes by leading an expedition of 13 armed ships to find the Spice Islands. On the way he put into the port of La Purificación on the coast of Mexico and was called inland to deal with an Indian revolt. With 100 cavaliers, Alvarado fell upon the Indians in the mountainous country north of Guadalajara. When they retreated to a hilltop, he followed on foot and flailed about with his sword. Just above him, a horse stepped on a pebble, slipped and fell on him. Within days, he was dead.

THE empire Alvarado had consolidated did not, however, die with him. As soon as they could, his successors tightened Spain's hold on the region. Inevitably, they imposed the rigid class system of Spain itself, with a few necessary modifications. The aristocrats were the *peninsulares*, men born in Spain, and usually officials sent to Central America by the king to rule in his name and look after his interests. Far below them were the *criollos*, those of Spanish blood unfortunate enough to have been born in the New World. They could acquire great wealth—and many did—but they were in general ineligible for the positions of greatest power. No *criollo* born in Guatemala could become a member of the Audiencia of Guatemala (the semijudicial, semiadministrative body which ruled the area in conjunction with the captain-general); nor could he become the captain-general. The highest position to which he could usually aspire was that of *corregidor*, a district administrator.

The third class consisted of the mestizos, men of mixed Spanish and Indian parentage. They were the small traders, the shopkeepers, the promoters. After them came the Indians and a group known as the mulattoes, the offspring of Negroes and Europeans, and the zambos, descendants of Negroes and Indians. At the very bottom of the social scale were the Negroes imported into the region to serve as slaves.

Originally, it had seemed unnecessary to bring in Negro slaves, for there were plenty of Indians at hand. But as prospective workers, the Indians had presented a considerable problem. In 1500 Queen Isabella had decreed that it was illegal to enslave them, and in 1537 Pope Paul III ruled that Indians had immortal souls. This was all very well except for the fact that the Indian would not work for the white man unless absolutely forced to. Regrettably, the *peninsulares* and the *criollos* had a distinct abhorrence of manual labor, for even if they or their fathers had come to Central America as foot soldiers, they now considered themselves hidalgos, gentlemen whose dignity permitted them only to fight and govern. Unfortunately for them, also, Negro slaves were difficult to obtain.

The solution to the problem of forcing the Indians to work without enslaving them was the encomienda system. Under it, the Crown entrusted a certain number of Indians to deserving Spaniards. The Spaniards received the right to use the Indians' labor; in return the encomienda holder pledged to look after their welfare—and especially their religious welfare.

In practice the solution proved no solution at all. The encomienda system quickly became indistinguishable from slavery. In 1520 Charles I abolished the encomienda, but protests forced him to restore it soon after. He abolished it again in 1542 and restored it again in 1545.

THE encomienda made life miserable enough for the Indians—but they also had to cope with the *corregidores de indios*. The *corregidores de indios* represented the Crown among the Indians, and almost without exception they represented it badly. They robbed the Indians of their produce and of their handicrafts, and sold the Indians' labor to Spaniards who did not hold encomiendas. The *corregidores de indios* set up shops in the villages and forced the Indians to buy at exorbitant prices products they did not want, did not need and could not use.

The only real protectors the Indians had were the distant Crown and the on-scene representatives of the Roman Catholic Church. Later the Church was to become rich and still later it was to become corrupt and cynical, but in the first century of the Spanish conquest of Central America, it devoted itself to saving not only the Indian's soul but his way of life and his well-being. At first the Dominicans were the outstanding champions of the Indians. Later the

Franciscans and finally the Jesuits became the most active missionary orders. None of them were invariably successful in gaining voluntary conversions among the Indians, many of whom accepted Christianity only because the alternative was death. There were others, however, who embraced the new faith without too much resistance, for they saw little contradiction between Christianity and their own religion. All the Maya tribes, for example, had held monotheistic ideas and a belief in an afterlife, and all had practiced the rite of confession.

BY and large, the early Spanish missionaries truly loved the Indians. The outstanding example was Bartolomé de Las Casas. An encomienda holder in Cuba who underwent a spiritual conversion in 1514 at the age of 40 after listening to sermons by a Dominican friar attacking the exploitation of Indians, he himself became a Dominican and was sent to Central America. Eventually named Protector of the Indians by his Church, he worked until the day he died at the age of 92 to deserve the title. Among other things, he kept the Crown constantly informed of abuses against the Indians.

Until Las Casas, the Spaniards had relied primarily on force to convert the Indians. Las Casas insisted that the Indians could be won by the Cross alone, and in 1537, according to a dramatic 17th Century account written by an admiring fellow Dominican, he was given a chance to prove his theory by converting an unconquered group of Indians living in a remote mountain cluster in Guatemala.

Las Casas first composed a group of ballads in the Maya language, recounting stories from the Old and New Testaments. Then he taught four Christian Indians to sing them. The Christian Indians went into the mountains, singing the ballads over and over. The Indians were enthralled. They asked for more information about this strange religion. Las Casas went into the mountains with several other Dominican friars and won the Indians to Christianity.

Unfortunately, when the Church became rich, it too began to exploit the Indians, for once it had land it also needed Indian labor. From there the step to corruption and cynicism was short.

It should not be imagined that every Spaniard who came to Central America, whether in armor or clerical robe, eventually amassed great wealth. On the contrary. Central America was poor in arable land as well as in gold. Only a few Spaniards actually held encomiendas and built great estates. The rest merely got along.

They grew maize, the staple of the Maya, and beans, on which the Maya also had lived. In the highlands, they grew wheat, in the lowlands sugar. Everywhere they grew fruit—apples and quinces in the interior of Guatemala, oranges and limes along the coasts. They raised cattle, horses and mules. Almost everything they produced, whether food or tobacco, cotton or wool, was intended not for export but for their own needs. The only major exceptions were hides, cocoa, and indigo, source of a blue dye then vastly popular in Europe. These were produced on the great estates, and they made the estate owners wealthy.

IN a colonial society intended only to enrich its masters, one would not expect to find much attention paid to cultural matters. This was not true in Central America. Although only an infinitesimal handful of men had wealth, they—and the Church—spent it lavishly on architecture, the arts and education. The Church in particular distinguished itself, first by composing grammars of the Indian languages and later by establishing seminaries which blossomed into universities open to laymen as well as priests. Until internal quarrels and opposition from the great landholders blocked its efforts, the Church spent a great deal of time in educating the Indian chieftains, several of whom made notable contributions to Central American culture.

Under the Spaniards, in fact, Central America produced great names: Bernal Díaz del Castillo, whose history of the conquest of Mexico is a classic; Quirio Cataño, the sculptor; Pedro Garci-Aguirre, the engraver; José Antonio Goicoechea, the physicist; José Felipe Flores, the physician.

Only in one art, in fact, did Central America lag—the art of politics. For unlike the English colonists in North America, the Central Americans never had an opportunity to govern themselves. They never were permitted to establish democratic institutions.

Independence found them incapable of governing themselves. And the inevitable result was chaos.

Two Indian girls, striped shawls over their heads, kneel before an altar in a Roman Catholic church in Comalapa, Guatemala.

Mellowing Relics of Spain's Long-gone Empire

Central America everywhere bears witness to the vanished power of its conqueror, Spain. In town and country houses, in fortifications and in churches, the skill and sensibility of Spanish artisans still shine forth. Showing the marks of Spain's own conquerors —the Moors—Spanish architecture is perfectly suited to the Central American climate. Easily adapted, too, was the Christianity the Spaniards brought. The local faith remains today a fascinating composite of Roman Catholic and Indian forms of worship.

PEDDLING WARES, Indians sell goods before the Church of Santo Tomás in Chichicastenango, Guatemala. Often, they burn incense to the old Maya gods before entering the church.

MAKING OFFERINGS, Chichicastenango Indians light candles to ask the aid of saints. If favors are not granted, the Indians sometimes punish the saint by placing his image in the rain.

STATELY TOWERS at each corner, a feature of certain cathedrals in Spain, ennoble the Sanctuary of Esquipulas in Guatemala. The church's striking Black Christ statue has made it a pilgrimage center.

GRACEFUL FACADE of a National University building (*opposite*) in Tegucigalpa, Honduras, although dating from the 19th Century, has a Spanish mood noticeable in the bell tower and the quiet plaza.

RICH DECORATION in a florid baroque style known as *churrigueresco (right)* embellishes the façade of the otherwise squat and massively built 17th Century Church of La Merced in Antigua, Guatemala.

*REMINDER of the past,
a 17th Century house
in Antigua, Guatemala,
recalls the colonial era*

CAVERNOUS KITCHEN in the Popenoe house *(right)*, an old Guatemalan domicile, contains shelves of crockery in a cupboard built into a vaulted wall. Its thick walls and strong roof enabled the kitchen to survive a disastrous 18th Century earthquake.

ARISTOCRAT'S PORTRAIT hangs on a wall with other period objects. They are part of a collection owned by Dr. Wilson Popenoe, an American horticulturist who bought the house in 1930 with his wife and restored it to its original condition.

ENORMOUS RECEPTION ROOM measures 90 by 92 feet *(below)*. In the right wall is a doorway to an inner courtyard on which all the principal rooms open. The walls on the street side are punctuated only by a few small, barred windows.

STATELY DINING ROOM has its own fireplace *(above)* and a portrait of the Virgin. One of the grandest of Antigua's homes, the house was built in 1634 by an aristocrat from Córdoba in a combination of Moorish and Renaissance styles.

53

Ragtag recruits to the forces of Carlos Castillo Armas struggle with the manual of arms in 1954 in Chiquimula, Guatemala. Castillo

Armas defeated the pro-Communist President Arbenz that year.

4

Early Unity and a Century of Disorder

HARDLY a shot was fired. There were no general uprisings, no army revolts. On September 15, 1821, Central America simply cast itself adrift from Spain.

In Mexico, Augustín de Iturbide, the rapscallion son of a wealthy Spanish father and a *criollo* mother, had raised the banner of revolt against the Government of the Spanish Viceroy. His aim, he said, was an independent Mexico, but one still paying allegiance to the Spanish Crown. When it became clear that his armed forces were going to be victorious, and when his political program, grandly labeled the "Three Guarantees," proved overwhelmingly popular, several of the Crown's own generals joined Iturbide, and the more prescient politicians in Mexico and Central America saw that Spanish rule was doomed. In Guatemala City the leaders of the clergy and others attached to the Captaincy-General —the old ruling body that governed the five provinces of Central America for Spain—met with a handful of great landowners and declared that Central America was independent, too. By this time, Spain was far from being the world power it once had been. It was, to a large degree, out of touch with its distant colonies and was quite impotent to raise and ship an army to face a revolt, however serious.

Iturbide crowned himself Augustín I of Mexico and invited the Central Americans to join his "empire." All the provinces that made up the Captaincy-General were willing to separate from Spain, but there was uneasiness at the prospect of joining Iturbide's Mexico. Many Central Americans feared that Mexico would assume Spain's role and begin running everybody's affairs. However, with Guatemala leading the way, Honduras, Nicaragua and Costa Rica fell in line and became parts of the Mexican "empire." El Salvador, on the other hand, refused to join Mexico. Infused with the republican spirit, its leaders were not about to exchange the King of Spain for a self-created "Emperor" of Mexico. But the military governor Iturbide had sent to Guatemala, a blunt soldier named Vicente Filísola, would have none of this, and after gathering an army, he invaded El Salvador in November 1822.

THE leaders of El Salvador at this point conceived the rather fantastic idea of becoming a part of the United States, and proclaimed themselves such. The United States was a dim and distant land, Protestant and English-speaking; but the United States was a republic, where men bowed to neither king nor emperor. El Salvador hurried to send an emissary to Washington to ask to join the Union.

Before this request could reach the United States, Filísola and his troops had entered the city of San Salvador. But almost before Filísola had achieved his victory, the Government for which he had fought had disappeared. A group of Iturbide's generals, led by Antonio López de Santa Anna (the same Santa Anna who later was to make Texas forever "Remember the Alamo!"), ousted Iturbide, who had been wildly extravagant with the young country's limited funds, and drove him into exile. When Filísola heard about all this, he hastily issued a decree justifying all his acts and reconvening the congress that had been called into existence by the Central American declaration of independence of 1821.

The National Constituent Assembly met in Guatemala City on June 24, 1823, and on July 1 issued a second declaration of independence, from Mexico as well as from Spain. At the same time, it established a loose confederation, the Provincias Unidas del Centro de América. Shortly before, Panama had declared itself independent of Spain, too, becoming part of Greater Colombia, which consisted of Venezuela, Ecuador and New Granada (as the present Republic of Colombia was then called).

THE Central American Federation lasted for 15 years. It was a triumph of rhetoric over reality, for there was no permanent capital, no army, no treasury to speak of and almost no way to raise funds. Not only were the provinces remote from one another, but within them, towns were separated by mountains and jungles and connected only by rude mule trails. Of a population of fewer than 1.5 million, perhaps only 100,000 citizens, mostly whites, could read or had much of any property. About 900,000 were Indians, some of whom worked on the big plantations, but most of whom lived off by themselves in tiny villages, so distant and isolated that they might have been on another planet. Another 450,000 were mestizos—part Spanish, part Indian; the remainder were Negroes and mulattoes. Racial differences, poverty, isolation, ignorance—none of these favored the creation of cohesive and informed bodies of citizens.

Worst of all, perhaps, since each province had developed separately from the others, the citizens of the Central American Federation had no sense of nationhood. A Guatemalan was a Guatemalan; a Costa Rican, a Costa Rican; a Nicaraguan, a Nicaraguan. No one was a Central American. Over the years, moreover, all the provinces had learned to hate each other and particularly to hate Guatemala, for in Guatemala lived the *peninsulares*—proud plantation owners who had been born in Spain—and Guatemala had been the seat of Spanish rule for centuries.

All, especially Guatemala, were torn by class war —between the *peninsulares* and the *criollos*, the wealthy landowners of Spanish descent who had been born in Central America, and also between the merchants and the professional men. These divisions were intensified by religious animosity, since the *peninsulares* upheld the privileges of the Church, while the *criollos*, by and large, were anticlerical.

LEADING FIGURES IN THE REVOLUTIONS AND REFORMS OF THE 19TH CENTURY

FRANCISCO MORAZAN   RAFAEL CARRERA   JUSTO RUFINO BARRIOS

THREE MEN dominated the history of Central America from 1830 to 1885. Morazán became President of the short-lived United Provinces of Central America in 1830. A liberal, he was deposed in 1838 by Carrera, who dissolved the United Provinces and ruled Guatemala for 27 years. After Carrera, an archconservative, died in 1865, a violent liberal reaction elevated Barrios to the presidency of Guatemala in 1873. Able if harsh, he promoted public works and broke the power of the Church.

The political leaders of the five former provinces did manage to write a constitution, but it was as fragile a document as the first U.S. constitution, the Articles of Confederation. It specifically declared each of the provinces "free and independent," and the federal congress was given power to legislate only in matters that concerned them all. The federal congress did not have the power to raise sufficient taxes; when in financial distress, it had to appeal to the provinces for contributions. The constitution abolished slavery and guaranteed free elections, but by restricting suffrage, it fixed control of the Government in the hands of the rich. It gave several guarantees of civil rights, but it restricted the right to worship in public to Roman Catholics.

The constitution had hardly been signed when the quarrels began. The first President, Manuel José Arce, took office in 1825 after a close and questionable election. Though considered a liberal of sorts, Arce immediately made the liberals angry by attempting to appease the conservatives. He then proceeded to infuriate the conservatives by pampering the liberals and ended up alienating almost every politician in the confederacy. He capped these unwise maneuvers by meddling in the affairs of Guatemala and Honduras. Uprisings broke out in 1826, and by 1827 the entire confederation was embroiled in a civil war. In 1829 Arce was forced to resign.

The liberals, who had marched on Guatemala City, put a 30-year-old Honduran, Francisco Morazán,

into the presidency. They then went to work to break the power of the Church, which had supported the conservatives. They abolished obligatory tithes, outlawed monastic orders, established freedom of worship and legalized civil marriages.

All of these liberal moves naturally infuriated both the conservatives and the Church. The situation was inflamed when, in 1837, an epidemic broke out. It was actually an epidemic of cholera, but the priests said the "godless liberals" had been poisoning the wells in order to wipe out the Indians and make room for European settlers. The Indians revolted, led by a 23-year-old Guatemalan mestizo named Rafael Carrera. Carrera was an illiterate. He was also a religious fanatic. His battle cry was: "Long live religion and death to the foreigners!"

Morazán defeated Carrera in skirmish after skirmish, but he could never destroy him. The war spread. Western Guatemala seceded from the confederation, setting up a new state called Los Altos. The congress decided in 1838 that any province could secede. Costa Rica, Honduras and Nicaragua did. Then the rest of Guatemala seceded, too, leaving only El Salvador. By 1840 Morazán, although he had won the battles, had lost the war, and he was exiled to Panama and then to Peru.

He returned, however, two years later at the request of the people of both Costa Rica and Nicaragua. Costa Rica was then under the iron rule of Braulio Carrillo. In 1841 Carrillo had declared himself the country's "perpetual" ruler, and now he was pressing a vigorous, if not always consistent or welcome program of reforms. He instituted attacks on the country's backwardness and distributed land among the peasants, but these reforms were supported by often cruel disciplinary measures. So the Costa Ricans who opposed Carrillo invited Morazán to land with an army, which he did in April 1842. This revolution was successful, but then Morazán, whose aim was to reunite all of Central America, made the mistake of attempting to conscript Costa Ricans for a march on Nicaragua and ultimately an attack on Guatemala City to oust Carrera. The conservatives, friendly to Carrera, organized a counterrevolution which was also successful. Morazán died before a firing squad on September 15, 1842, the 21st anniversary of Central America's first declaration of independence.

Today, Morazán is a hero throughout Central America. In his native Honduras, there are monuments to him wherever one turns. For Central Americans now agree that he was a true democrat who sought to break the power of the Church not because he was "godless" but because he opposed all special privilege. Equally important, they now agree that it was a tragedy for Central America that Carrera's revolt against Morazán destroyed the Provincias Unidas del Centro de América.

THE breakup of the confederation set the pattern of Central American history for more than a century. Rafael Carrera was the first of the strutting men. He was, despite his semiliteracy, a surprisingly efficient administrator. He gave Guatemala a stable and honest Government. He built roads; he encouraged agriculture. Yet at the same time, he was a despot who loved the gaudy trappings of power. Privately, the clergy and the great landowners deplored him as a barbarian—but they supported him, nevertheless, because he not only repealed all the liberal anticlerical laws, restoring the power of the Church, but time and time again he launched wars against liberals elsewhere in Central America to put conservatives in office. Quite frequently the men he put in office did not stay there very long. Once his armies had left, the liberals would drive them out again. In 1848 the liberals even managed to drive Carrera himself from Guatemala City. However, the liberal victories were always temporary; Carrera always came back. His strength lay with the Indians, who remained loyal to him. They called him *Hijo de Dios,* "Son of God," and *Nuestro Señor,* "Our Lord."

As a result, for a quarter of a century, until his death at 51 in 1865, Carrera dominated not only Guatemala but Honduras, Nicaragua and El Salvador as well, protecting the privileged. The Pope decorated him for his services to Catholicism, as did Santa Anna of Mexico for his services to conservatism.

HEARTENED by Carrera's death, the liberals surged back. One by one, conservative strongholds fell to liberal armies. In June 1871, Guatemala City itself fell, and in 1873 Justo Rufino Barrios became ruler of Guatemala. Like Carrera, he was a mestizo, but unlike Carrera, he had little sympathy for the Indians and encouraged European immigration. He was as ruthless as Carrera and as fanatically anticlerical as Carrera had been pro-Church. Just as Carrera had made war throughout Central America to maintain the power of the conservatives and the Church, so Barrios made war to destroy it.

In Guatemala, Barrios exiled the Jesuits, the archbishops and bishops; outlawed tithing and religious processions; closed monasteries and convents; confiscated the properties of the orders; made civil marriage obligatory; forbade priests and nuns to wear clerical garb in public and barred them from teaching. In place of the Church's system of parochial schools, he established a system of public education.

Again like Carrera, Barrios did much to improve the country, building roads, founding banks and encouraging agriculture. He was not content with this, however, for his ambitions extended far beyond Guatemala's borders. El Salvador and Costa Rica had liberal Governments, but they were not ruthless enough for him. He especially disliked Tomás Guardia, the liberal President of Costa Rica. Guardia had smashed the Costa Rican oligarchy, distributed much of its land among the peasantry, and embarked on a vigorous program of internal development. He had done nothing to suppress the Church, however, and for this Barrios would not forgive him. But despite every kind of underhanded maneuvering, Barrios could not dislodge Guardia. Barrios was far more successful in his efforts to seat liberal governments elsewhere. In 1876 he went to war against both El Salvador and Honduras and succeeded in putting a Government to his liking in power in both countries. Seven years later, he again intervened in Honduras when the man he had put in power earlier proved intractable. Again, Barrios was successful. Two years after that, in 1885, he decided to restore the Central American Federation with himself as supreme chief.

At first glance, the political situation appeared to favor Barrios' plan. Not only were El Salvador and Honduras now ruled by Governments that he himself had set up; in Costa Rica, Guardia had conveniently died. His successor, Prospero Fernández, was a man after Barrios' heart. He had exiled the Jesuits, suppressed the other religious orders and established public schools. Nicaragua's Government was conservative, but not militantly so.

Barrios failed to reckon with the intense nationalism that had destroyed the confederation in the first place. Only Honduras fell in with his plan; the other nations prepared to fight. Barrios marched into El Salvador at the head of his Army, but in one of the first engagements he was mortally wounded.

After Barrios, the history of Central America is a history of chaos. Dictator followed dictator. Some called themselves liberals, others conservatives; actually, none cared for anything except power. Some were reasonably good administrators. Most devoted every waking moment to larceny. Almost without exception, they were murderers as well as thieves. None managed to extend his sway beyond his own country as Barrios (and Carrera before him) had done. Perhaps the most notorious of all was Manuel Estrada Cabrera, who became the President

---

CONTINUING BORDER DISPUTES

Territorial disputes born in the 19th Century have endured into the 20th in Central America. Below are two of the noteworthy cases.

MOSQUITIA: This wedge-shaped region of some 7,000 square miles extending inland from the east coast of Nicaragua and Honduras has been argued over by the countries since 1858. Under a treaty signed between them in 1894, a boundary commission was to settle as much of the border as it could and leave the rest to an impartial arbitrator. The arbitrator immediately chosen by the commission was Alfonso XIII of Spain, who in 1906 awarded almost all of Mosquitia to Honduras. Nicaragua accepted the award but in 1912 declared it null and void, mainly on the grounds that the treaty had specified that the commission first attempt to find an arbitrator from the Guatemala City diplomatic corps. The issue remained relatively quiet until 1957, when Honduras began extending its administrative control over the region. Nicaragua sent troops into the area; scattered fighting broke out. After a cease-fire, the International Court of Justice in 1960 upheld Alfonso's award.

EL SALVADOR-HONDURAS BORDER: Although efforts to delineate the frontier began in the mid-19th Century, a section is still contested. Lands belonging to a number of villages along the border and a number of islands in the Gulf of Fonseca remain in dispute.

---

of Guatemala in 1898. Cabrera remained in power for more than two decades, winning farcical rigged elections in 1905, 1911 and 1917. He was finally declared a mental incompetent by the Guatemalan congress (which was given moral encouragement by U.S. President Woodrow Wilson) and was swept from office in 1920. Cabrera worshiped himself, making his birthday and his mother's birthday national holidays. He kept the Indians in peonage and looted the national treasury.

After his overthrow, Guatemala enjoyed several years of constitutional government. Then in 1931 Jorge Ubico came to power. He was an ascetic, hard-working and scrupulously honest man (at least where other people were concerned) who spent hours every day poring over Government records to discover whether any bureaucrat had been stealing. Ubico's concern for the honesty of others did not prevent him, however, from making himself an enormously wealthy man. He became the biggest individual landholder in Guatemala during the 13 years of his presidency. His official salary was $28,000, but he is said actually to have averaged some $156,000 a year.

Ubico was a fanatic on the subject of sanitation. Under his dictatorship, Guatemala City became one of the cleanest cities in the world. Ubico posed as a friend of the Indians and outlawed peonage. He balanced the budget and brought modern highways and airports to the country. He would sometimes test the country's roads on his own motorcycle, and if he discovered a bumpy spot, he would find the official in charge, take away his car and make him ride a bicycle for a year. At the same time, however, he decreed that people could be forced to work for the Government if they failed to pay taxes. In effect, this made the Indians peons of the Government. An excellent boxer in his college days, he would challenge a subordinate and beat him up. He reinforced a slight resemblance to Napoleon by affecting a Napoleonic haircut, and he aped the gestures of that earlier admirer of both violence and order.

The people of Guatemala suffered under Ubico's eccentric but total dictatorship for 13 years. Slowly, however, resistance began to form, and in 1944 the people struck for their political rights. The revolution, when it came, was instigated by students and members of the armed forces. Ubico went into exile, ending up in New Orleans, where he died in 1946.

Elsewhere in Central America the story has been essentially the same. Honduras has had so many dictators that it is almost impossible to count them. Until Tiburcio Carías Andino fought his way into office in 1933, they followed each other with bewildering rapidity. Carías Andino was an Indian, a mountain of a man with a thick, white mustache, who lived in such fear of his life that when he attended Mass his Army set up machine guns inside the cathedral. He filled the jails with political opponents, and his precautions were justified. Almost every man in Honduras lived in the hope of killing him. But he managed to survive and retired voluntarily in 1948.

The blackest of all the dictators in Nicaragua's history was José Santos Zelaya, who became President in 1893. He called himself a liberal; he was, in fact, a homicidal maniac who tortured and killed his opponents, looted his countrymen and, not content with that, sold what he could of his country's resources to foreigners. Like Barrios, he dreamed of becoming dictator of all Central America. He kept stirring up revolts wherever he could until the U.S. Government conspired with his opponents to oust him.

ALMOST without exception, El Salvador's dictatorships were mild, if not benevolent. The revolutions were brief and often bloodless. They rarely occurred except when the great landowners quarreled with each other. Since the landowners were often related, their fights were like family quarrels, but family quarrels punctuated by gunfire.

Compared with the history of the rest of Central America, Costa Rica's is relatively orderly. Most of the cultivated land is worked by small, independent farmers, growers of sugar and coffee. Those not living in the area near the capital live in physical isolation from one another. In addition, the whole country, because of the mountains on the northern border, lives in comparative isolation from the rest of Central America, separated by both geography and desire from the other nations' constant turmoils.

The people also have had in the past little sense of nationhood. In the early 19th Century, Costa Rica was, in effect, four nations, each centered on a city: Herédia, Cartago, San José and Alajuela. Only a handful of wealthy Costa Ricans cared about politics, and their only political concern was the orderly preservation of the status quo. Order was so easy to achieve that, as early as 1848, they decided it was unnecessary to have an army, although they maintained an elaborate civil guard.

IT happened nowhere else in Central America, and it has rarely happened anywhere in the world: strangely, in Costa Rica, dictatorship evolved into democracy. The man who began this evolution was Tomás Guardia, the erratic reformer of the 1870s. Guardia was not an advocate of democracy, except in name, but he gave Costa Rica a democratic constitution. It remained a scrap of paper throughout his life; however, three years after Guardia's death, Bernardo Soto made it a reality. Soto, who became President in 1885, established a system of public education which has made the Costa Ricans by far the most literate of all the Central Americans. And, when his term expired, Soto not only got out of office and held a free election, but he also accepted the verdict, even though it went against the candidate he had backed.

Soto's example did not save Costa Rica from occasional dictatorships, but it established a precedent. Ever since, Costa Ricans have taken democracy seriously. They will even fight for it, as they did in 1948 when an allegedly Communist revolutionary group sought to prevent Otilio Ulate, the legally elected President, from taking office.

Unfortunately, Costa Rica is unique. The other Central American nations have never experienced democracy long enough to appreciate it, much less understand it. To them, democracy is a word—and an accident.

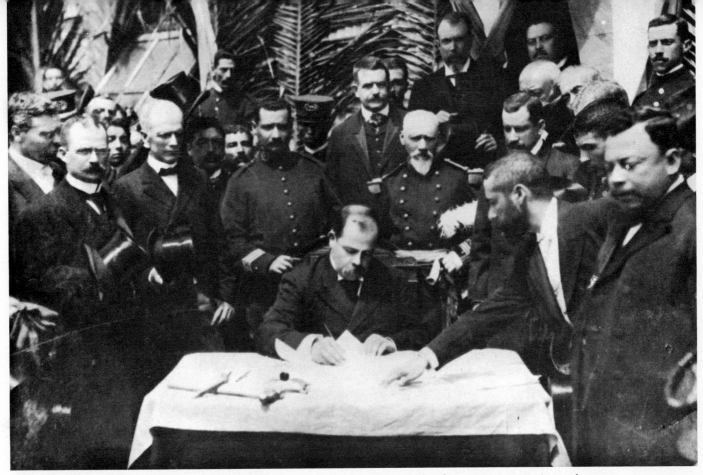

With aides, Manuel Estrada Cabrera, who ruled Guatemala with the help of secret police from 1898 to 1920, signs a document.

Chronic Conspiracy and Repeated Revolt

Conspiracies, coups, revolts and wars have been endemic in Central America. Governments tend to change with bewildering rapidity; since 1821, when Central America became independent from Spain, dictator has followed dictator in most of the republics. Further, the various countries have among them written in that time at least 45 different constitutions. More than once the United States has felt impelled to step into the area's affairs—and as a result has earned a still-existing legacy of bitterness. Recently, the area's chronic poverty, which has been the ultimate cause of so many past revolts, has made it fertile ground for Communist subversion.

DAPPER STRONGMAN, General Jorge Ubico, President of Guatemala from 1931 to 1944, visits an Indian village during a tour of the country. Ubico was a ruthless but effective ruler.

DEEP GORGE known as the Culebra Cut is dug by U.S. engineers in 1909. The nine-mile channel had to be blasted through mountains; 128 million cubic yards of dirt and rock were eventually hauled out.

INSPECTION TEAM of U.S. officials, accompanied by wives and children *(right)*, pauses by one of the Canal's immense locks. The Canal swarmed with official guests and tourists during its construction.

NOTED VISITOR, President Theodore Roosevelt takes the controls of a giant steam shovel *(left)* during an inspection tour in 1906. It was his leadership that was responsible for the Canal's being dug.

RUSHING WATER begins to fill one of the locks at the Pacific end of the 50-mile waterway *(below)* before the Canal was opened in 1914. The gates of the locks are seven feet thick and six stories high.

*U.S. MARINES intervened
in Nicaragua to put down rebellions
and protect U.S. interests*

ORGANIZING A PATROL, mounted Marines dress ranks *(above)* in the town square of Ocotal, Nicaragua, in 1928. Marines were in Nicaragua almost continuously from 1912 to 1933.

CLEARING A TRACK, Marines remove a barrier from a Nicaraguan rail line in 1912. They had landed to put down a rebellion against President Adolfo Díaz, who was friendly to the U.S.

GRIPPING HIS GUN BELT, the Nicaraguan rebel leader Augusto César Sandino registers defiance in one of his mountain hide-outs. Sandino led a guerrilla war from 1926 to 1933.

BEATING OFF AN ATTACK in 1912 *(below)*, a group of Marines fires on rebels who have been seeking to oust Díaz. The U.S. action caused frequent charges of "dollar imperialism."

WAVING A SWORD, a Sandino lieutenant, Manuel María Jirón, strikes a brave pose. An honest, U.S.-supervised election ousted Díaz in 1928, but Sandino and Jirón continued to fight.

65

ILL-FATED PRESIDENT, Jacobo Arbenz *(wearing jacket)* talks with a Guatemalan Communist. A leftist, Arbenz was overthrown by Carlos Castillo Armas, who was backed by the U.S.

DISSIDENT SOLDIERS fire on supporters of Castillo Armas during a brief counterattack by disgruntled Army officers following Castillo Armas' invasion from his Honduran exile.

GUATEMALAN UPHEAVAL in 1954
deposed a pro-Communist Government
and focused world attention on the country

VICTORIOUS REBEL, Castillo Armas *(at microphone)* makes his first speech in Guatemala City. Despite his personal honesty, his Government proved to be graft-ridden and unpopular.

STUDENT RALLY in Honduras *(left)* protests Castillo Armas' invasion of Guatemala. The pro-Arbenz students display signs attacking United Fruit and invoking the hero Sandino (page 65).

LOYAL TROOPS guard the residence of President Juan B. Sacasa of Nicaragua in 1936 against attacks from "Tacho" Somoza's National Guard. Somoza won, becoming President in 1937.

COSTA RICAN MILITIA stands watch against attacks from Nicaragua in 1955 in a short war precipitated by mutual dislike between Somoza and Costa Rica's President José Figueres.

CONTINUING VIOLENCE *plagues*

UNIVERSITY STUDENTS in Guatemala City *(left)* hold a mass meeting in 1956 to plan anti-Government demonstrations with the aim of overthrowing the regime of Castillo Armas.

INFANTRY PATROL moves up on a farmhouse in Nicaragua to hunt guerrillas who had infiltrated from Costa Rica in 1959 to overthrow the regime of Luis Somoza. He had succeeded to the Nicaraguan presidency after the assassination of his father in 1956. The 5,000-man Nicaraguan National Guard, to which these men belong, is the best-trained force in Central America.

Freighters enter the Miraflores Locks at the Pacific end of the U.S.-controlled Panama Canal to begin the trip that will take them across

The Involvement of the U.S.

5

Central America to the Atlantic. Each year more than 11,000 ships make the voyage through the 50 miles of channels, locks and lakes.

THERE is a popular notion that Central America has been largely ignored by the most powerful nation of the Western Hemisphere. In point of fact the United States has been involved for more than a hundred years in Central American affairs, in part because of its own interests, in part because of the manifold activities of an oddly assorted group of Americans dedicated both to enriching themselves and to a belief in the "Manifest Destiny" of the United States.

No one still talks about Manifest Destiny, but there was a time in the mid-19th Century when everyone did. Most Americans appeared to believe that it was God's will that His country should carry the blessings of American democracy to the far shores of the Pacific and even to Central America; in the years before the Civil War, there were Southerners who actually clamored to make Central America part of the United States. The U.S. might have invaded Central America at that, except for one factor: the South insisted that the greatest of all the blessings of American democracy was slavery, and the North, already embroiled in conflict with the South over that issue, thought it had trouble enough. Even so, a young Southerner named William Walker came close to making Nicaragua safe for slavery, after first making himself President of the country. Together he and another strong-willed man, "Commodore" Cornelius Vanderbilt, succeeded in keeping Nicaragua in turmoil for years.

A third American, Minor Cooper Keith, built a web of railroads through Central America, making the banana industry possible; he accumulated so much wealth and power that he became known as the "uncrowned king of Central America." A fourth, Sam Zemurray, converted bananas into an "empire of green and gold." Still another American, Theodore Roosevelt, created the Republic of Panama, ordered the completion of the Panama Canal, and thereby made a reality of the long-held dream of a westward passage to the Pacific by sea.

AMERICANS had been seized by that dream during the 1846-1848 war against Mexico, which culminated in the acquisition of California. In 1847 George Law, a New York builder, obtained a Congressional subsidy to carry mail from New York to New Orleans and to what is now the city of Colón, at the mouth of the Chagres River on the Caribbean coast of Panama. At the same time, a New York steamship man, William H. Aspinwall, was granted another subsidy for the operation of a line from Oregon and California to Panama. The plan was to connect Law's line and Aspinwall's by canoe and mule.

No one expected Law and Aspinwall to make a great deal of money from the operation, but the ink was hardly dry on the contracts when gold was discovered in California. Immediately, both Law's and Aspinwall's steamship lines themselves became gold mines. Law was able to charge $500 for a berth, and in 1849 his line earned a profit of three million dollars. Aspinwall did as well, for despite the cost, the trip to California via Panama was far swifter than the overland journey across the continent.

It was by no means an easy trip. After passage in a crowded, foul-smelling stateroom, the gold seekers had to climb down rickety ladders into frail canoes at the mouth of the Chagres. Often they lost all they possessed going ashore in the tricky waters. Once ashore they faced greater trials: a miserable ride up the Chagres and a perilous journey to Panama City across the Isthmus, a trip on which they were tormented by sunstroke, fever, insects and brigands.

In New York, Cornelius Vanderbilt enviously watched the "forty-niners" pouring aboard Law's ships. A big, brawny fighter of a man, who had already amassed a fortune by gaining control of most of the ferries and steamboat lines around New York City, Vanderbilt had never been one to ignore the possibility of making a dollar. He conceived the idea of building a canal across Nicaragua, which would cut the journey from New York to San Francisco by 500 miles and enable him to take all of Law's business.

Vanderbilt, however, was not alone in his interest in a Central American canal; the U.S. Government was actively considering treaties with several Central American governments for the construction of one. So, too, were the British, for Lord Palmerston, the British Foreign Minister, was convinced that an American-owned canal would inevitably give the U.S. a stranglehold on British commerce. Neither nation, however, wanted a collision with the other, the British in part because they feared the loss of their American cotton supplies, the U.S. because of the continuing slavery crisis. In consequence Sir Henry Lytton Bulwer and Secretary of State John M. Clayton signed a treaty in 1850 agreeing that neither the U.S. nor Britain would ever attempt to construct a canal over which either would have exclusive control.

THE Clayton-Bulwer Treaty, which remained in force until 1901, was a victory for Britain but not truly a defeat for Vanderbilt. He created three corporations: the Nicaragua Steamship Line to carry passengers to Nicaragua, the Nicaraguan Canal Company to dig the canal under joint Anglo-American management and the Accessory Transit Company to carry passengers across Nicaragua while the canal was under construction.

Vanderbilt's engineers, however, assured him that his plan for transporting passengers up the San Juan River and into Lake Nicaragua, and thence overland to the Pacific, was not feasible; dangerous rapids, they said, made the San Juan impassable. Vanderbilt was unimpressed. He set sail for Nicaragua, trailing a river boat, the *Director,* behind his ocean-going steamship *Prometheus.* At the mouth of the San Juan, he took over the helm of the *Director* and drove her upriver, crying for steam. After 119 miles of rapids and rocks, he brought the *Director* safely into Lake Nicaragua.

His engineers were convinced. Then Vanderbilt started a rate war against Law. Fares went steadily down until a man could get to Nicaragua in steerage for $45. In one year alone, Vanderbilt's Nicaragua Steamship Line and his Accessory Transit Company took in a two-million-dollar profit. The profits, however, were to be short-lived, for Nicaragua was soon to be torn asunder by the activities of the strange young Southerner named William Walker.

Today, Walker's name lives on in Central America as a synonym for infamy. Oddly, he came originally to Central America as a liberator. The poet Joaquin Miller was to say of him later that William Walker had "a princely air, a presence like a chevalier." Horace Greeley was to call him "the Don Quixote of Central America." Both were right. William Walker was both incandescent and preposterous.

CORNELIUS VANDERBILT, who began to amass his fortune by founding a New York ferry line, early conceived the idea of digging a Nicaraguan canal. It was never dug, but the "Commodore" made millions shipping "forty-niners" to the Isthmus.

Walker was born in Nashville in 1824. A small man who never weighed more than 120 pounds, he studied medicine at the University of Pennsylvania and was graduated at 19. He pursued medical studies in Europe, and then became a lawyer in New Orleans.

The law, however, was not for Walker either. He switched to journalism, becoming an editor of the New Orleans *Crescent.* As a journalist, he was a radical, advocating among other things the right of women to vote. As a Southern journalist, he never dared to come out for the abolition of slavery, but he made it clear that he detested the institution.

William Walker was unquestionably a man of ideas and ideals when he started on his adventures.

What he became later is another question, one to which historians cannot find an answer. A firm believer in the Manifest Destiny of the United States, he believed that it was *his* destiny to spread the "blessings of American democracy"; in all likelihood he also hoped that by doing so he would divert his countrymen from the ruinous civil war toward which they were thundering.

Walker's first attempt to spread the blessings of American democracy was an effort to make the Mexican state of Sonora "an independent republic" under the protection of the United States. With 45 men, he invaded Lower California in 1853, intending to invade Sonora from Lower California. He succeeded in taking the peninsula, but his conquest had an unexpected effect. The United States had long been attempting to buy northern Sonora from Mexico. The U.S. Minister to Mexico, James Gadsden, had offered $10 million for the land. Mexico had scornfully rejected the offer, but when the Mexicans heard of Walker's invasion of Lower California, they panicked and sold northern Sonora to the U.S.

This transaction, known as the Gadsden Purchase, added some 45,000 square miles to the territory of present-day New Mexico and Arizona, but it simultaneously destroyed Walker's hopes of "liberating" southern Sonora. For, having gained what it wanted from the Mexicans, the United States decided to cooperate with them. It did everything it could to keep Walker from getting reinforcements and supplies. He managed to launch his invasion of Sonora, but without ammunition and food his force disintegrated, and he was forced to retreat.

Destiny, however, soon called again. Ever since the breakup of the Central American Federation in 1838 (see Chapter 4), Nicaragua had been in turmoil. In six years the country had been subjected to 15 presidents, with the liberal Democrats alternating with the aristocratic Legitimists. The capital had shifted back and forth between Granada in the south, the stronghold of the Legitimists, and León in the north, where the Democrats held sway. Now, with the aid of the British, the Legitimists had gained the upper hand. The Democrats still held León, but they were a force under siege. At Britain's urging, the Costa Rican Government had joined the struggle on the side of the Legitimists.

William Walker's adventure in Lower California and Sonora had ended in disaster, but it also had made him a hero to Central American liberals. In 1854 the Democratic rebel government called on him for help. Walker rounded up and outfitted 58 men, chartered a leaky brig and landed in Nicaragua in June of 1855.

Within months newspapers everywhere in the world would acclaim Walker and his men as "the Immortals." A Paris journal would compare him to George Washington. Indians would hail him as a liberator. Yet his first days in Nicaragua were dark, for he made what he soon discovered was a serious mistake by accepting reinforcements from the Democrats. They were conscripts who would not fight. In his first clash with the Legitimists, the conscripts fled, leaving "the Immortals" outnumbered 10 to 1. "The Immortals" killed 10 to 1, but they, too, were finally forced to flee.

"GENERAL" WILLIAM WALKER, a fiery American journalist, invaded Nicaragua, conquered it and had himself elected President. Eventually forced out of the country, he reinvaded Central America twice. In 1860 he was executed in Honduras.

Fortunately for Walker, he found an ally shortly afterward, an Indian named José Vallé, who offered to round up a volunteer force of Indians. With Vallé's volunteers, Walker was able to muster a force of some 250 men. Under cover of darkness, he stormed the Legitimist capital of Granada and captured it, almost without firing a shot.

But, still fearful of American control over Central America, the British intervened, and armed the Costa Ricans to fight. Faced with this threat, Walker sought to unite Nicaragua by forming a coalition Government of Democrats and Legitimists. When the coalition fell apart, he called for elections, ran for the presidency—and won, to the near-unanimous applause of the Nicaraguans.

Shortly after his moment of triumph, however, Walker found himself beleaguered again. This time he was to meet his match. Before leaving on a European tour, Cornelius Vanderbilt had left his Nicaraguan enterprises in charge of two agents whom he thought he could trust, Charles Morgan and Cornelius K. Garrison. Neither, however, proved particularly trustworthy. In his absence they gained control of Vanderbilt's Accessory Transit Company through stock manipulations and purchases and then, in an effort to ensure stability in Nicaragua and protection for their investment, presented Walker with a gift of $20,000 and a vague offer of troops. Infuriated, Vanderbilt immediately began reacquiring control of the company by stock purchases of his own. Counterattacking, Morgan and Garrison persuaded Walker to seize the company and turn it over to them in return for a promise to give the Nicaraguan treasury a larger share of the company's profits. Vanderbilt thereupon entered the alliance against Walker, dispatching two well-financed agents to Central America, plus a consignment of Minié rifles and ammunition. Day by day Walker's desperation increased. At this moment, while the U.S. teetered on the brink of the Civil War (which was to break out four years later), former Senator Pierre Soulé of Louisiana came to him. His Southern friends, Soulé told Walker, were prepared to give him men, arms and money if he would legalize slavery in Nicaragua. Walker, who had started his career as a critic of slavery, accepted the offer. And now the Nicaraguan Indians turned against him, too.

Soulé was, however, unable to make good on his promises. After the Royal Navy prevented the Southern reinforcements dispatched by Soulé from landing in Nicaragua, two columns of Costa Rican troops, one commanded by a Vanderbilt agent and armed with his rifles, the other by a British Army captain, marched against Walker. Other Central American nations attacked, too. Garrison and Morgan deserted the cause. Overwhelmed, Walker finally surrendered himself into the custody of the commanding officer of an American warship, which returned him to the United States. Walker's departure, however, brought no success to Vanderbilt. The affairs of Accessory Transit subsided into a tangle of claims, counterclaims and litigation, and the whole grandiose scheme for a Nicaraguan canal eventually collapsed.

Walker made two further attempts to conquer Central America. In the first, he staged an invasion of Nicaragua but was stopped by a force of two British and two U.S. warships and 300 U.S. Marines. In the second, he landed in Honduras, hoping to join forces with a rebel movement. This time he was captured by the British and handed over to a Honduran firing squad. On the morning of September 12, 1860, Walker told a priest, "I am prepared to die. My political career is finished," walked to a wall and faced the firing squad. He was 36.

WALKER failed to create an empire in Central America; the United Fruit Company succeeded. Compared with General Motors, General Electric or American Telephone & Telegraph, United Fruit is today not too imposing a corporation by American standards; by Central American standards it is a giant. There was a time in Costa Rica, for example, when the national budget was not as large as that of United Fruit; in some of the republics, United Fruit for years was the major source of revenue, and whenever the governments went into the red, it was "the banana company," as Central Americans still call it, that extended loans to make up the national deficits.

United Fruit is no longer el pulpo (the octopus) whose tentacles reached deep into economies and governments and by its power altered them at its will. It has become a highly enlightened company, which endeavors to avoid meddling in politics. Yet the legacy of hatred survives. To Central American leftists, United Fruit remains a whipping boy.

The men who created the company envisioned no such outcome. Most were interested not in power but simply in profit. There was Carl Augustus Frank, a German-born ship's steward who developed a taste for bananas when his ship docked at Colón and who, with his brother Otto, started the first regular banana trade between Central America and the United States in 1864. There was Lorenzo Dow Baker, a tall, sallow Yankee sea captain who took 160 bunches of bananas aboard his schooner *Telegraph* one day in 1870 as a gamble, sold them 11 days later in Jersey City at a profit of two dollars a bunch and went into the banana trade full time. There was Andrew Preston, a Boston clerk who came across Baker's bananas in 1871, tried one, found it delicious and offered Baker a deal: let Baker bring the bananas to Boston and Preston would sell them.

THE man who did more than any other to create United Fruit, however, was a youngster from Brooklyn named Minor Cooper Keith. In 1870 he was invited by his brother Henry Meiggs Keith to help build a railroad to link the interior of Costa Rica to the Caribbean. Young Keith rounded up 700 laborers in New Orleans and set out for Puerto Limón. On arrival, he and his men found the town a rainy swamp, swarming with mosquitoes. Within a week, half of Minor's workers were down with malaria and yellow fever. The two brothers also contracted malaria but somehow kept going. They survived, but 600 of the 700 men Minor had brought with him from New Orleans did not. With Jamaican laborers who proved relatively immune to malaria, the brothers pushed on with the railroad. Henry Meiggs Keith died; Minor took over and sent for his younger brother Charles. By then the Keiths had managed to put down approximately 60 miles of track.

Nevertheless, they were desperately in need of money. If they could find freight to carry along that 60 miles, they would have money coming in—but where in that drowning jungle wasteland could they find freight? Minor was confident that he could grow bananas in the jungle. He went to Colón and obtained several hundred root bits.

Charles died, too, but Minor did not give up. He planted bananas and, with the money he got for them, continued to put down railroad ties. The banana plantations spread throughout Central America and so did the railroad. By 1899 Keith was the biggest banana grower in Central America; in that year he went into partnership with Baker and Preston to found the United Fruit Company. He let Preston run the company and continued to build railroads. By 1912 he was running a network of roads that extended through El Salvador and Guatemala to Mexico. At his death in 1929 he was preparing to push the network south to Panama City.

To Keith, Baker and Preston, bananas were basically freight and profit. Sam Zemurray, who started as a rival of United Fruit's and wound up as its president, was a farmer who liked to grow bananas.

A banana trader from Alabama, he first bought acreage in Honduras in 1905. Later he acquired other land in Honduras which everyone, including the United Fruit Company, had long agreed was probably the best banana land in all of Central America but which everyone had refrained from buying because the title was unclear. Zemurray solved the problem by paying off both claimants to the land.

Compared with the United Fruit Company, Zemurray's Cuyamel Fruit was a pygmy. But thanks to Zemurray's genius as a farmer, it soon became the most productive grower in Honduras. United Fruit recognized Zemurray's talent, and in November 1929, shortly after Minor Keith's death and just one month after the U.S. stock-market crash, it acquired Cuyamel in a stock deal. Zemurray became the largest stockholder in United Fruit as a result.

FOR a while Zemurray simply enjoyed his dividends. But as the Depression deepened, Zemurray's stock fell. On top of that, sigatoka, a fungus that destroys the banana leaf, swept Central America. The disease threatened to wipe out the banana industry and, with it, not only United Fruit but much of the economy of Central America. In 1932 Zemurray utilized his position as the major stockholder to assume active control of the company. Under him, United Fruit managed to destroy sigatoka with chemical sprays. The company also introduced broadscale mechanization; banana production climbed and so did employment.

Paradoxically, however, United Fruit was trying to free Central America from its bondage to bananas.

In 1925 it had begun experimenting in Panama with the growing of abacá, or Manila hemp, the fiber that is used to make the ropes and hawsers vital to naval and merchant shipping. By 1941 the company had 2,100 acres planted in abacá, and when early in World War II the Japanese seized the Philippines, the U.S.'s only other source of supply, the company gave the Government its entire seedbed and agreed to plant, without profit, another 20,000 acres in abacá. United Fruit then began to plant abacá in Costa Rica, Honduras and Guatemala, an action that helped to save the Central American economies during the war, when most of the company's "Great White Fleet" was taken over by the U.S. Navy and shipments of bananas and other commercial crops to North America and Europe became few and far between. Restored to the company after the war, the Great White Fleet now numbers 52 vessels.

IT was an earlier, smaller war that brought the U.S. Government into direct involvement in the affairs of Central America. That conflict, the Spanish-American War of 1898, was like World War II a two-ocean war, and the U.S. no more possessed an effective two-ocean fleet then than it did at the outset of World War II. The Navy was forced to dispatch the battleship *Oregon* from the Pacific for action in Cuba by way of Cape Horn, a dangerous voyage that took more than two months. The troubles of the *Oregon* brought home to Americans the realization that a Central American canal was essential to American security.

The idea of a canal was of course not new, as we have seen. Long before Cornelius Vanderbilt launched his abortive effort in Nicaragua, the U.S. Government had begun studying the feasibility of a canal. All studies had recommended that one be dug through Nicaragua, taking advantage of the San Juan River and Lake Nicaragua route which Vanderbilt and others had considered. In 1897 President William McKinley gave the project high-level support, declaring that a Nicaraguan canal was "indispensable to that intimate and ready intercommunication between our eastern and western seaboards demanded by the annexation of the Hawaiian Islands and the prospective expansion of our influence and commerce in the Pacific." At the same time, French

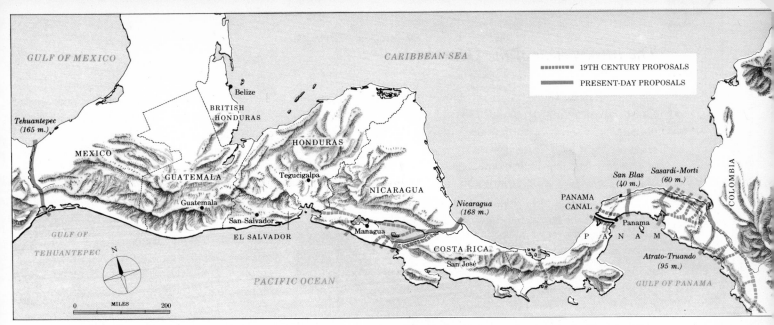

Map labels:
GULF OF MEXICO · CARIBBEAN SEA · 19TH CENTURY PROPOSALS · PRESENT-DAY PROPOSALS · Belize · BRITISH HONDURAS · HONDURAS · Tehuantepec (165 m.) · MEXICO · GUATEMALA · Tegucigalpa · NICARAGUA · Guatemala · San Salvador · EL SALVADOR · Managua · Nicaragua (168 m.) · San Blas (40 m.) · Sasardi-Morti (60 m.) · PANAMA CANAL · Panama · COLOMBIA · GULF OF TEHUANTEPEC · COSTA RICA · San José · PANAMA · Atrato-Truando (95 m.) · PACIFIC OCEAN · GULF OF PANAMA · N · MILES 0 200

ALTERNATIVE CANAL ROUTES, including those proposed in the 19th Century before the Panama site was chosen, and those suggested today for a second cut, are shown above. The present-day proposed routes, with their mileages, are shown as planned for digging by conventional methods. If nuclear blasting is used some routes might be slightly altered, since atomic explosions would make some short cuts possible. Nuclear blasting is believed to be less expensive than conventional digging.

interests were urging the U.S. to abandon plans for a Nicaraguan canal and to purchase the properties of a French company which had taken over the assets of a predecessor. The original French company had acquired from Colombia the right to dig a canal across the Isthmus of Panama, an area then part of that country. It had begun construction and then abandoned the project.

The French valued their Panamanian holdings and rights at $109 million; a U.S. commission appointed to look into the canal question refused to recommend payment of more than $40 million. But in 1902, after a disastrous volcanic eruption on Martinique in the West Indies, lobbyists for the French company sent every U.S. senator a copy of a Nicaraguan postage stamp showing a Nicaraguan volcano in full eruption. One of the French lobbyists later asserted that $60,000 had been donated to the Republican Party in an effort to enlist the support of Senator Mark Hanna, the G.O.P. power. Be that as it may, the Republican-dominated Congress passed a bill in June of 1902 which provided that President Theodore Roosevelt, McKinley's successor, pay the French $40 million for their Panamanian rights if suitable treaty arrangements could be made with Colombia. If not, the President was to proceed with plans for a Nicaraguan canal.

Early in 1903 the U.S. Secretary of State, John Hay, negotiated a treaty with a Colombian representative under which the United States agreed to pay Colombia $10 million for the French rights and, eventually, a yearly rental of $250,000 for a strip of land six miles wide across the canal route.

The Colombian congress held out for more money, failed to get it and rejected the agreement. Roosevelt was not amused. "Those contemptible little creatures in [Colombia]," he had growled to Hay, "ought to understand how much they are . . . imperiling their own future." Then, as he put it later, Roosevelt "took the Isthmus." In essence, what he did was to back a "revolution" in Panama by elements anxious to see the U.S. build a canal there—or, at least, he ensured the revolt's success by preventing Colombia from suppressing it. To that end he dispatched the U.S. gunboat *Nashville* to Colón. On November 3, 1903, some 500 troops and two generals sent by a worried Colombian Government disembarked in Colón and requested transport to Panama City over the French-owned rail line, which was then operated by American engineers and personnel. Warmly, the Americans dispatched the generals and their staffs to Panama City, promising to send on the troops when sufficient rolling stock, then mysteriously absent, showed up. In Panama City late that afternoon, the generals were placed under arrest by one General Esteban Huertas, who had been bribed to do so for $50,000. This act constituted Panama's revolt against Colombian rule. Two days later the

77

500 men left in Colón returned home under the command of a bribed colonel ($8,000).

On November 6, three days after the revolt had broken out, the United States recognized the independence of Panama. Construction operations on the canal commenced within the year.

As a creature of the United States, Panama not only accepted the terms that the Colombian congress had rejected, but went further: it approved a treaty whose wording declared that the United States was to exercise total sovereignty in perpetuity over a 10-mile-wide strip across the Isthmus. Panamanian governments have contended ever since that Panama retained actual sovereignty over the land. Whatever the merits of the dispute, the Canal was opened to world commerce on August 15, 1914.

The dream of the westward passage at last had been achieved, more than four centuries after Columbus, but the treaty that made the Canal possible still plagues relations between the United States and Panama. Under it, the Panama Canal Zone has become a country within a country, a prosperous, gleaming suburb of the U.S. set between Panama City and Colón. Although the squalor to be found in both cities is hardly the fault of the U.S., the contrast between the Zone and the slums of Panama has a strange psychological effect on the Panamanians: it makes them angry not with the Panamanian leaders who are basically responsible for their misery but with the Zonians and with the U.S. Unfortunately, both the Zonians and the U.S. constantly aggravate this anger. The Zonians never hesitate to make it clear that they consider the Panamanians an inferior race, and the U.S. frequently treats Panama like a colony.

THE treaty and the Canal were not the only legacies Roosevelt left to American posterity. He also made the Monroe Doctrine anathema throughout Latin America in general—and Central America in particular—by promulgating what came to be known as the Theodore Roosevelt Corollary to the Doctrine. It had become customary for the Central American republics and for such Caribbean nations as Haiti and the Dominican Republic to borrow money from private bankers and then neglect to repay it. The U.S., argued Roosevelt, was morally obligated to collect such loans for European bankers since,

under the Monroe Doctrine, Europeans were barred from using force to collect the money themselves.

This reasoning quickly became an integral part of U.S. foreign policy. Under the Theodore Roosevelt Corollary, the U.S. on several occasions landed Marines in Honduras and Costa Rica. For years the Marines actually ruled Nicaragua.

The Marines first took over Nicaragua in 1909 to restore order after a revolution in which two Americans had been killed. In 1911, at the request of the U.S. Government, two New York banks granted Nicaragua a loan. Under the agreement, the banks were given control of Nicaragua's finances. When a revolution swept the country in 1912, imperiling the regime of President Adolfo Díaz, who had made the agreement, Díaz and the banks called on the U.S. for help. The U.S. sent in the Marines again. This time they were to remain for 13 years.

IN 1914 the United States signed a treaty with Nicaragua. In return for a paltry three million dollars, the Nicaraguans granted the U.S. the right in perpetuity to build a canal across their country, a 99-year lease on the Corn Islands in the Caribbean and the right to maintain a naval base in the Gulf of Fonseca. The broad privileges granted by the treaty were breathtaking—but understandable. By then Nicaragua had become a virtual colony of the United States. Marines were stationed in Managua, the capital; Americans and American agents collected the customs duties; Americans ran the national bank.

A year after they left the country in 1925, the Marines returned, again at the invitation of President Díaz, to suppress a revolt brought against him by dissidents who called themselves the "Liberals." The Liberals' social program was vague; their primary aim was to rid Nicaragua of American influence. In 1927 Henry L. Stimson, acting as the representative of President Calvin Coolidge, brought the revolt to an end with the promise that the United States would supervise the next two Nicaraguan presidential elections—those of 1928 and 1932. Both, oddly enough, were won by Liberal candidates. In the interim, however, the campaign to oust the Americans was taken up by a Nicaraguan general, Augusto César Sandino. The U.S. called Sandino a "bandit and murderer." But to the overwhelming majority of Central

Americans, Sandino was a hero. In 1925 Sandino had thrown in his lot with the Liberal revolutionaries. He formed a guerrilla army and carried on the fight after the Liberals had accepted the Stimson compromise. From 1927 until 1932, 5,000 U.S. Marines and 2,500 Nicaraguan National Guardsmen trained by the Marines unsuccessfully pursued Sandino through the Nicaraguan jungles.

When the Marines were finally recalled in 1933, in accordance with the terms of the Stimson agreement of 1927, Sandino laid down his arms. On February 21, 1934, President Juan Sacasa invited Sandino, his family and several of his political cohorts to dinner at the presidential palace to discuss the future of Nicaragua. Leaving the palace, Sandino, a brother and two friends were seized by National Guardsmen. They were thrown into a truck, carted to the Managua airport and slain by machine gunners.

Many Central Americans insist that Sandino had agreed to dine with Sacasa only because the U.S. Minister to Nicaragua, Arthur Bliss Lane, promised him safe-conduct. There is not an iota of evidence to support this, but in Central America it is not difficult to find people willing to believe the worst of the U.S.

Franklin D. Roosevelt's Good Neighbor Policy made the Theodore Roosevelt Corollary obsolete, but the Cold War later gave the U.S. an imperative reason for intervention in Central American affairs.

On March 15, 1951, Jacobo Arbenz Guzmán became President of Guatemala. An Army officer and a landowner but a leftist in his political thinking, he entered into a coalition with the Communists, who rapidly gained control of the labor movement and took dominant posts in the Government.

NOT only the U.S. was seriously worried. Guatemala's next-door neighbors, Honduras and El Salvador, were also concerned. They feared that, having gained a foothold in Guatemala, the Communists would now attempt to seize power throughout Central America. It was not an unreasonable fear.

The U.S. Government mounted plans to overthrow Arbenz. It had a willing instrument in Carlos Castillo Armas, a former colonel in the Guatemalan Army who had gone into exile in Honduras and, with the help of the Honduran Government, was attempting to raise an army of exiles to fight Arbenz. Castillo Armas was not a particularly able man, but he was honest and well meaning. The Defense Department started arming and training his men, and gave him four old F-47s, World War II fighters capable of carrying light bombs.

THEN word came that a Swedish freighter, the *Alfhem*, was heading for Guatemala with a load of Czechoslovakian arms. To this day it cannot be said for certain why Arbenz wanted the arms. Perhaps he wanted to strengthen his Army against Castillo Armas; perhaps he wanted to create a militia of workers and peasants. The U.S. Central Intelligence Agency believed he wanted the arms to invade Honduras and Nicaragua. On June 18, 1954, Castillo Armas' small force crossed the Honduran frontier.

The "Liberation Army" could easily have been contained if the Guatemalan officer corps had been willing to throw the Guatemalan Army into full-fledged action. But Guatemala's colonels were also concerned about the Communist threat; many were also convinced that Arbenz did intend to create a militia that would not be subject to Army control.

It is commonly said that the U.S. toppled the Arbenz regime; a more accurate statement would be that it administered a well-timed shove. The major engagement of the war, in which 17 men were killed on both sides, was won by the rebels on June 24. The following day, moreover, the F-47s managed to terrify Arbenz' supporters by dropping a few bombs on Guatemala City. The U.S. Government has consistently denied it, but it is known that these raids, as well as other parts of the U.S. intervention, were planned by the late John E. Peurifoy, U.S. Ambassador to Guatemala, and the late Whiting W. Willauer, U.S. Ambassador to Honduras. Simultaneously, Peurifoy told Arbenz' colonels that he, too, believed that if Arbenz managed to suppress Castillo Armas' revolt, the Army sooner or later would be replaced by a militia. The colonels abandoned Arbenz. On June 27 Arbenz resigned, and on September 11 he was permitted to leave the country.

It was, in a way, a great coup for the United States. Yet it was by no means to bring about an amelioration of the conditions which had enabled an Arbenz to come to power in Guatemala, nor of those which beset the rest of Central America.

BANANA PLANTATION owned by U.S. Standard Fruit Company stretches along a road in Honduras, where men and mules plod to work. Standard has vast holdings in Central America.

INTENT STEVEDORE takes hold of a box of bananas *(above)* as other boxes roll aboard ship at the port of La Ceiba. Honduran agriculture is dominated by large U.S. fruit companies.

Agricultural Economy Tied to U.S. Markets

The fortunes of the six Central American republics remain bound up with the United States. The involvement has ceased to be obviously political: Marines no longer land to "pacify" revolutions, and robber barons no longer march in to obtain sweeping concessions for themselves. But economically Central America is still closely linked to the colossus to its north, for the area's economy remains primarily agricultural, and the United States remains its major market. The U.S. imports $200 million worth of Central America's products—mainly coffee, cotton and bananas—each year, and big U.S. companies like United Fruit and Standard Fruit have a total investment in Central America of $350 million.

MODERN PACKING PLANT of Standard Fruit in Honduras *(left)* washes "hands" (clusters) of bananas and sends them on conveyor belts to be rewashed, cooled and boxed for shipment.

HAND LABOR remains a basic part of the area's underdeveloped agriculture

PICKING COFFEE, two children balance on ladders on a Panamanian plantation to reach the ripe red berries which contain the beans. Berries must be carefully picked, for one tree produces only a single pound of marketable coffee each year.

SORTING COPRA, dried coconut meat, a group of women *(opposite)* work on the floor of a drying shed in El Salvador. The copra is pressed to produce an oil used in making oleomargarine, cooking oil, other food products and cosmetics.

CHECKING COCONUTS, a worker watches a hopper from which the nuts drop to be conveyed to a dehusking machine. The production of copra is being experimented with in Central America by the well-to-do Salvadoran Benjamín Sol.

COFFEE of high quality is grown
in each country. It constitutes
the area's most important single export

BAGS OF BERRIES are dumped into a vat to be washed *(above)*, the first of several steps in which the skin and inner pulp are stripped from the two coffee beans inside the berry.

PLANTATION WORKERS transport coffee berries *(above)* on a *finca* at Antigua, Guatemala. World coffee prices have been low, and even fine Guatemalan coffee brings small profit.

ACRES OF BEANS still covered by a final jacket of yellowish, parchmentlike skin are turned *(below)* by workers to dry in the sun. Tombs in Antigua's graveyard gleam in the distance.

PROCESSING COMPLEX of the San Lázaro coffee *finca* near Antigua forms a compact pattern from the air. Coffee exports make up 10 per cent of Guatemala's gross national product.

EXTENSIVE GIN YARD, where seeds are removed from cotton fibers, stretches toward the volcano of Usulután in El Salvador. The gin is on the land of Juan Wright, a leading planter.

MIGRANT FIELD HANDS who pick cotton for Juan Wright wait in line *(below)* for their evening meal. More than 60 per cent of El Salvador's work force is employed in agriculture.

WHITE MOUNTAIN of cotton waiting to be ginned is piled up at the cooperative by pickers. Compared with the U.S.'s cotton output, that of El Salvador and its neighboring countries is minuscule. However, more land is being put into cotton, and modern farming techniques are now being introduced. Cotton is also stimulating the growth of a local textile industry.

BANANA PICKERS leave a plantation at La Ceiba, Honduras. They earn about $3.50 a day, a figure above the Central American average. Yet jobs on the plantations are increasingly difficult to find and the Honduran cost of living is high.

The Landless Poor

A DAY or two after President John F. Kennedy outlined his plan for the Alliance for Progress in 1961, the wife of a San Salvador banker descended on a visiting American businessman at a diplomatic reception. "I always knew that Kennedy was a Communist," she said, "and now he's proved it." Taken aback, the American asked the lady what she meant. "Why, don't you understand?" she said. "That man wants to give everything we have to . . . to . . . to . . . those animals with names."

The outburst, of course, revealed more about the banker's wife and the thinking of the ruling groups of Central America toward the Indian citizens of their countries than it did about Kennedy or the

Alliance, that high-minded offer of aid to South American Governments if they themselves would undertake economic reforms. More than 400 years have passed since the conquistadors enslaved the Indians, but the legacy of the conquistadors remains. To most of the oligarchs who replaced the *peninsulares* as the ruling class when Central America became the United Provinces (see Chapter 4), the Indians and mestizos still are simply "animals with names."

For, despite the marching and countermarching of the dictators and would-be dictators, the bloodshed and the turmoil, Central America has never experienced a lasting social revolution. And even though slavery was outlawed by the constitution of the

United Provinces, it has persisted in one form or another until recent years. Until 1934, for example, Guatemalan Indians labored under laws which permitted the owners of *fincas,* or coffee plantations, to lend them money and then demand work in payment of the debt. Since wages paid on the *fincas* were barely enough to keep the Indians alive, they never were able to pay off their debts. The Indians remained in bondage until they died. Their children inherited the debts and in their turn became slaves of the *finca* owners.

After 1934 Guatemala instituted a vagrancy law which brought even more Indians under control. Under the provisions of the vagrancy law, any person who did not have a trade or a profession, or who was not cultivating specific amounts of land, was required to work for some employer for 100 to 150 days a year. In practice, this included virtually every Indian in Guatemala, and the law remained in effect until 1944.

Today, the Indians face other problems. Under age-old Indian custom, a father almost invariably hands down his land to his elder sons; the others must leave it. The younger family members have very little choice: they can swarm into the cities, where jobs for them are scarce, or else they can seek work from the *finca* owners. If the *finca* owner employs them, he may pay them as little as 80 cents a day. Moreover, the work is seasonal for some; when the crop is harvested, the Indians are forced to move on. Indians who obtain jobs as *colonos,* or resident workers on the *fincas,* are somewhat better off. The *finca* owner gives a *colono* the use of a hut and a patch of ground on which to grow vegetables and keep chickens, and he is required by law to provide schooling for the worker's children.

Actually, the Indian who gets a job on a *finca* is fairly lucky. In recent years, a number of wealthy Guatemalans have been turning land into cotton. The cotton planters, by contrast with the coffee planters, do not bother to provide more than limited shelter for the Indians they hire. Considerably better off are Indians who obtain jobs on United Fruit's plantations. United Fruit provides schools for its workers' children and housing superior to that found on many *fincas,* and its hospitals contain some of the best medical facilities in Guatemala.

As for the Indian who goes into the city, his is a life of complete despair. There are few jobs for him. Unable to read and write, knowing little except the technique of growing maize, he can offer an employer nothing except his back. He may have a slightly better chance of obtaining work if he is a "Ladino," i.e., a person who has accepted the white man's language and customs and abandoned those of his ancestral village. In the struggle to gain a measure of economic well-being, the Ladino's chances are far better in the long run than those of the Indian who follows the ways of his ancestors. But for the moment the streets swarm with Indians and Ladinos alike attempting to stay alive by peddling lottery tickets or by shining shoes.

At that, there are not many shoes to shine. The last complete Guatemalan census, taken in 1950, reported that less than a quarter of the population above the age of seven wore shoes and that most of those who did were Ladinos. Only some 3 per cent of Indian men and 2 per cent of Indian women wore shoes; slightly more than 27 per cent of the men and 5 per cent of the women wore sandals; 69 per cent of the men and 93 per cent of the women went barefooted. This was not because the Indians and the Ladinos preferred the comfort of bare feet; they could not afford sandals, much less shoes. The situation has improved since 1950, for Guatemala's economy is booming. Nevertheless, it is obvious

---

THE ALLIANCE FOR PROGRESS

The U.S.-proposed Alliance for Progress program envisages no less than an economic and social revolution. To receive U.S. aid, the Central American countries, like their neighbors, pledged not only to spend funds of their own but, among other things, to undertake programs to wipe out illiteracy, carry out land and tax reform, assure fair wages, stimulate private enterprise and encourage economic integration. During the fiscal year 1963-1964, the U.S. committed $105.6 million to such Alliance programs in Central America. Some of the funds went to private and governmental banks and lending institutions for loans to develop private industry, the remainder into rural development, education and public health. During the late 1960s, the bulk of the funds will be spent to encourage economic cooperation and integration.

even to the most casual observer that shoes remain beyond the means of a majority of Guatemalans—and the overwhelming majority of Indians.

Many wealthy Guatemalans insist on pointing out that "the Indians really don't want much. They're not like us. They're a religious people, with little desire for material things." The point is well taken; the Indians are not overly interested in the white man's trappings.

BUT whether or not the Indian is content with his poverty, he certainly does not look forward to dying any more than anyone else does, nor to watching his children die. And the death and disease rates among the Guatemalans are appalling, in part because virtually no medical care was given the Indians until this century. Guatemalan doctors were more concerned with keeping epidemics among the Indians from sweeping into the cities than with eradicating the causes of epidemics. Energetic campaigns against disease, largely financed by the Rockefeller Foundation, have been carried on in more recent years. Even so, in 1962, the last year for which statistics are available, there were 17.3 deaths for every 1,000 inhabitants, compared with 9.4 for every 1,000 in the U.S. The principal causes were gastroenteritis and colitis, pneumonia, bronchitis and tuberculosis, malaria, influenza, worms, whooping cough, measles and dysentery.

Poor and diseased, the Guatemalans are illiterate as well. Only 30 per cent of the population can read and write. Among the Indians, fewer than 10 per cent are literate. The problem of educating the Indians is complicated by the fact that many of them cannot speak Spanish. In addition, many wealthy Guatemalans do not believe in educating Indians, and many Indians see no particular point in becoming literate: knowing how to read and write will not do a man much good if the only job open to him is picking coffee berries. Yet the situation may not remain stable forever. One longtime American resident of the country recently told a visitor that he had decided to stop growing cotton. "In the first place," he said, "just because it's a big money-maker, everybody's going into cotton; we'll soon have overproduction. More important, though, I'm convinced that sooner or later the workers on the cotton plantations are going to explode. You can't exploit people as the cotton planters are exploiting them without having an explosion. Sooner or later, the unions will go into the cotton fields, organize the workers and call the damnedest strike you ever saw."

The Guatemalan story is paralleled throughout Central America (except in Costa Rica). Everywhere, the lower classes are regarded as "animals with names." Only the statistics differ. Nicaragua has, for example, a substantially lower infant mortality rate than Guatemala, but even there the rate is shocking (54.3 deaths for every 1,000 live births, compared with 91.3 for Guatemala and 25.3 for the U.S.). El Salvador has a lower rate of illiteracy than Guatemala, but even in El Salvador 58 per cent of the people cannot read and write.

The statistics spring to life when one visits the slums of Managua, San Salvador, Guatemala City, Panama City or Colón. In the Central American countryside, the colorful costumes, the religious rituals, the music, the dance camouflage the squalor. The slums are squalor unadorned. Perhaps the worst slums are those of Panama City and Colón, if only because of the contrast they make with the manicured Canal Zone. Well over half of the families in Panama City live in one room in wooden houses, many of them visibly falling apart. Some of the houses were built when the Canal was being built.

IN the one-room apartments lives an average of almost four persons. In many of them live eight or 10. They are not big enough for eight or 10 beds, of course, and some of the apartment dwellers sleep under the beds and some of them sleep in hammocks slung over the beds. It is a rare apartment that has its own toilet, and at least 50 per cent of the families of Panama City and Colón share a toilet with others. It is an even rarer apartment that has a kitchen. The inhabitants cook in the same room in which they sleep. They do their laundry in that room, too, although most of the houses do not have running water; the inhabitants carry water from a tap in the patio. Garbage, reeking in the sun, creates an overpowering stench.

The people manage to obtain just enough to eat to keep going: for breakfast, a couple of slices of bread or a couple of tortillas with black coffee; for lunch, a soup or a dish of rice and meat; for supper, a dish of rice and beans. Occasionally, there is a can of condensed milk for breakfast; sometimes lunch is a dish of rice and dried shrimp; sometimes a bit of meat or shrimp is mixed with the rice and beans at dinner.

Panama has a very special problem, what might be called a lower lower class, the West Indian Negroes. One might have expected that Panama, a potpourri of races, would have developed a high degree of racial tolerance, as Hawaii did. For many years the opposite was true. All but a handful of Panamanians have at least traces of Indian or Negro ancestry, or both, yet men were long measured by the exact shade of their skin or by the kinkiness of their hair—or, to put it another way, by how Caucasian their features seemed. By such standards the West Indians were placed at the very bottom of the social scale.

In 1941, under the presidency of Arnulfo Arias, the pro-Nazi, a new constitution was enacted which stripped citizenship from Panamanians of West Indian ancestry who could not speak Spanish, and prohibited the further immigration of West Indians into Panama. Arias justified this action by insisting that the admixture of West Indians with Panamanians "drains the strength of the race." Citizenship was later restored to these native-born Panamanians, but the prejudices were of course not totally eradicated.

THERE are various reasons for such intolerance. One is the need of every depressed human being to find someone he can feel superior to. In a sense, the Panamanian lower classes were like the white Southern sharecroppers in the U.S. who are most intolerant of Negroes. The attitude of some Panamanians is reinforced by the fact that a number of West Indians, even those born in Panama, cannot speak Spanish or else speak the language with a perceptible West Indian accent.

Although the situation is altering for the better today—color is a handicap against notable success in business, government and the professions, but not an absolute bar—there are still Panamanians who resent the fact that a very high proportion of the West Indians work in the Canal Zone, where they draw higher wages than Panamanians working in Panama. (The West Indians, of course, originally came to Panama to work on the Canal because the Panamanians themselves could not or would not.)

The United States must bear a good part of the blame for the Panamanian attitude. American race-consciousness visibly accentuated Panamanian race-consciousness over the years. Although desegregated today, the Zone was originally as strictly segregated as Mississippi.

ONE of the results of the degradation in which the lower classes of Central America live is the high rate of illegitimacy. Former President Ramón Villeda Morales of Honduras frequently remarked that 70 per cent of the children of his country were born illegitimate. Except in Costa Rica, the figures are comparably high elsewhere. The reason is not, as popularly supposed, the high cost of marriage. The cost is not that high. The problem apparently is that a meaningful family life is almost impossible for many Central Americans.

Among small landowners, common-law marriage is quite prevalent, and such liaisons appear just as stable and enduring as those blessed by law and religion. In fact, among small landowners, it is not unusual for a dying man to marry the mother of his 14 children on his deathbed.

Marriage of any kind is a rarity among landless workers and in the slums of the cities, however. Landless men frequently are itinerant workers who move from place to place, even from country to country, leaving illegitimate children behind them. In the slums of the cities, sex is a public affair. Men and women have relations in front of children, and the children grow up regarding sex as they regard eating.

Yet despite the general social miseries which overlie much of Central America, the fact remains that it is unnecessary for the vast majority of its people to live and die in squalor. And the proof is Costa Rica.

Costa Rica is not a paradise. The growth in population runs neck and neck with the growth in the gross national product. Per capita income in 1962 was only $290. A small drop in the price of coffee can shake the economy. Costa Rica, like the rest of

Central America, has landless farmers. It has farmers with too much land and farmers with too little.

However, Costa Rica has enough farmers with enough land on which to live to give many people better than a subsistence living. One such farmer, for example, is a man we shall call Manuel Rivera, who has some 25 acres planted in potatoes, carrots and beans near Cartago, in central Costa Rica. Rivera rents the land from two uncles, and he hopes eventually to inherit it. He has another five acres in maize not far away which he farms in partnership with one of his cousins.

With his wife María and three children—two boys of eight and two, and a girl, six—Rivera lives in a semi-old, semi-new farmhouse of five rooms. The older section has thick plaster walls and a red tile roof; the newer has concrete walls and a corrugated iron roof. Both sections stand in vast contrast to the "ranchos" in which live the Indian farmers of Guatemala, for example, which are mostly dirt-floored huts with thatched roofs. The Rivera home has electric lights and a refrigerator, an electric stove and running water—which does, however, sometimes fail in the dry season. María hopes to persuade her husband to buy a television set next year "for the children's sake."

ON the Rivera farm, day begins with first light and a breakfast of black beans, rice and coffee, and, perhaps, fried plantains. The older boy walks half a mile to the main road and then catches a bus to school in Cartago. The six-year-old girl attends school in the nearby village and next year will join the boy in Cartago. While they are away, María works on her household chores, sometimes assisted by a girl from the village. Laundry is done in the back yard, in a deep cement sink and a couple of galvanized washtubs. Lunch is similar to breakfast, but meat—veal, beef or tripe—comes with the evening meal. The family is usually abed by 8 o'clock.

Manuel, too, has help, two more or less permanently employed farm hands who average about $1.25 a day and are given lunch. At harvesttime he augments the staff to six. At present he owns a jeep, which the family uses for occasional trips to town, but no tractor. He is thinking of buying a secondhand tractor whose cost, he believes, could be easily taken care of by rentals to neighbors. At present he rents a tractor, and gathers his crops in an old-fashioned, two-bullock oxcart whose ironshod wooden wheels are painted in the traditional gay designs. Like many a man elsewhere, he tends to be reticent about his income, but he probably averages between $100 and $150 each year. In a bumper year, he might double that amount, but in a bad year his income might be cut in half.

AT 32, Rivera is better off than many Costa Rican farmers, but not by very much. Small farmers like him are to be found virtually all over Costa Rica. In more remote areas, farmers are without electricity and possibly without running water, and a good proportion of Costa Ricans in Rivera's economic bracket are sharecroppers or tenants. And of course, there are members of the upper classes in Costa Rica who are far more well-to-do than he or his hired men. He and farmers like him constitute about 20 per cent of the Costa Rican population.

Yet the average Costa Rican farmer does not live in a hut, but in a frame house. It may not be large (it is usually about the size of the weekend summer cottage of a worker in the U.S.), but it is substantial. It is painted. It is spotless inside; outside it is framed in flowers.

The Costa Rican farmer is just as proud and self-reliant as the New England farmer. He knows what is happening in the world because he can read: 80 per cent of the Costa Ricans are literate; a considerable number of them have been to college.

Most important of all, perhaps, Costa Ricans like Manuel Rivera have definite ideas about what the Government should or should not do, and they know how to make their views felt. As a result, the Costa Rican Government is reasonably sensitive to human needs. The country not only has an extensive educational system; it has an extensive hospital system as well. The Costa Rican death rate is one of the lowest in Central America: in 1962, the year Guatemala had 17.3 deaths for every 1,000 inhabitants, Costa Rica had 8.5.

Most wealthy Central Americas are quite unmoved by the example of Costa Rica. Mention it and they will say, "Yes . . . but, as you know, the Costa Ricans are white."

A water boy peddles his merchandise in Masaya, Nicaragua. The lack of sanitary facilities in poor districts contributes to the spread

The Festering Problem of the Poverty-ridden

The Central American Governments frequently announce programs to deal with the circumstances—lack of education, agricultural economies dependent on fluctuating world prices, inadequate medical care—that combine to perpetuate the area's poverty. Yet land remains concentrated in the hands of a few; poor roads keep villages in isolation and hamper the movement of goods and the opening of new

of disease, a problem compounded by the scarcity of medical care.

UNEMPLOYED WORKERS pass the time in Portobelo, Panama. Long a thriving port, the town declined in importance after it was bypassed by the Panama Railroad, which was built in 1855.

SKIPPING CHILDREN play in a Portobelo Negro slum. Negroes were first imported to build the Panama Canal. Today, about 75 per cent of Panama's citizens have Negro ancestry.

areas. A population growth rate that is among the world's highest offsets economic gains. Respiratory and intestinal diseases are major killers; aspirin is the universal specific, and it sells for 10 cents a tablet. Yet even though Central Americans are poverty-stricken in material matters, arts, skills and a feeling for beauty evolved out of centuries of tradition lend warmth to lives spent amid conditions of squalor.

AT SCHOOL, a Guatemalan Indian girl *(opposite)* ladles soup into her bowl. Free schools are available in theory, but more than 60 per cent of Guatemalan children never attend classes.

AT HOME, a Cuna Indian girl of Panama's San Blas Islands swings in a hammock. With their tribe living in virtual isolation, few Cuna Indian children ever see the inside of a school.

THE RITUAL OF THE MARKET attracts traders in Santiago Atitlán, Guatemala. Each Indian arrives early to pick a spot to display his leatherwork, textiles, vegetables or other goods, and by 10 a.m. the market is in full swing. Few buy early in the day, however, except tourists who do not know better, because the traders love to bargain. They feel that the most

expert bargainer is the best customer, and most transactions are made near closing time, just before the trader would have to carry his merchandise back home. Since the Indian never considers the cost of his labor, he is satisfied if at the end of the day he has made 25 to 50 cents, out of which he must pay local authorities a tax of several cents for the use of his space.

NATIVE SKILLS, now disappearing, survive in villages and in the work of Indian painters

HAND WEAVING on a primitive loom *(opposite)* is practiced by a young girl in Masaya, Nicaragua. The Indians still use hand looms for weaving small textiles, which may take months to complete, but larger pieces are often made on foot looms in village weaving centers.

VILLAGE SCENES are painted by Andrés Curuchich *(right)*, who uses the same bright hues favored by weavers. Curuchich, an Indian house painter, still works at his trade in Comalapa, Guatemala. His paintings have been exhibited in the United States as well as in Europe.

LOCAL LANDSCAPE of San Antonio del Oriente, Honduras *(below)*, was painted by an Indian barber, Antonio Velásquez. To the right is a portion of the scene depicted in the painting. The Indians have only recently begun to realize the commercial value of their arts.

7

The Great Families

THEY are called by a variety of names: the Catorce Grande, the Veinte Familias, the Rabiblancos. No matter what the name, they are the families that own Central America, the oligarchs. By American or European standards, even by South American standards, they are not staggeringly wealthy. Most of the men are not even millionaires. Only in El Salvador is there a millionaire *class*. Except for the Somoza brothers, who run Nicaragua in tandem, it has never been possible for any family to accumulate what a Rockefeller or a Rothschild would call a real fortune. The countries are too small, too poor. In Central America a man who is worth five million dollars is a Croesus. The Somozas are among the most powerful of the oligarchs, because Tachito Somoza runs the Nicaraguan army, as his father Tacho did before him, and the Somozas thus control the country's military as well as much of its financial power. So large is the clan today that almost every business of any size has over the years acquired a Somoza partner. Tacho never made any bones about his methods: "We Nicaraguans are a Spanish and Indian mixture and that's dynamite," he once said. "Give us a finger and we take a hand. Give us a hand and we take an arm."

The Somozas at present control about one tenth of the cultivable land in Nicaragua—and just about everything else worth owning. The country's only airline is theirs, as is the only television station, a newspaper, a cement plant, a textile mill, several sugar refineries, half a dozen breweries and distilleries, a metalworks and even a Mercedes-Benz agency. Their fortune is estimated at between $150 million and $350 million; the family income is said to be about one million dollars a year—in a country where the average per capita income runs to about $250.

THE Somozas are, of course, an extreme case. In none of the other Central American nations does a single family own as much of the economy as they. In all the Central American republics, however, a handful of families generally dominates the economy. By doing so, they dominate Central America because there are no other power groups. In the United States, by contrast, there are tens of thousands of associations that can bring pressure to bear on government—both local and national—and on big business. There are labor unions and PTAs, farm organizations and chambers of commerce, consumer groups and chapters of the League of Women Voters. These groups vary as widely as the American Farm Bureau Federation, the John Birch Society and Americans for Democratic Action. Money talks in the United States no less than in Central America, but in the U.S., labor also talks, the farm bloc talks, even garden clubs and sewing circles have a voice in local affairs. There are times when money cannot make its voice heard above the babble.

It is taken for granted in the United States that the farmers in a remote corner of a rural county will succeed in making the local government repave their road when it falls into disrepair. It is likewise taken for granted that unions have the power to gain from industry, year after year, pay raises and more generous pension plans. On a national level, it was possible for enthusiastic Republican voters to nominate Barry Goldwater for President in 1964 despite the determined opposition of the wealthy "Eastern Establishment" of the Republican Party typified by Governors Rockefeller and Scranton, both heirs to vast fortunes accumulated by oligarchic families.

None of these things could or do happen in Central America. There the oligarchy of moneyed families can rule relatively unhindered because a multitude of power groups, as in the United States, simply does

not exist. The Indians cannot organize politically; they lack both the leadership and the money. Since Central America has relatively little industry, the labor unions are small and therefore weak. The farm bloc and the oligarchy are one. The Church has limited influence because, in the 19th Century wars between liberals and conservatives, the liberals destroyed the power of the Church. There are only two real forces in Central America: the oligarchy and the army. Usually, although not always, the army is officered by, and has served as the handmaiden of, the oligarchy.

The situation will change only when Central America develops a measure of industry and, with it, a skilled, educated working class and a middle class. These will become countervailing forces of the kind the United States possesses. Until that happens, however, a handful of families will continue to dominate Central America both economically and politically.

How many of these families are there? The question causes endless discussion and debate all through Central America, but it is simply impossible to answer. For the oligarchic families are so few that, unless their children marry Americans or Europeans, they have to marry each other; the result is that in each country most of the families are interrelated. For example, many of the members of El Salvador's Catorce Grande (literally, Big Fourteen) insist that the upper class of El Salvador consists of perhaps 100 families, not, as the name implies, just 14. On the other hand, a member of one of these families once haughtily told a U.S. correspondent: "We are not fourteen families; we are five." It depends on how one pigeonholes in-laws and cousins twice removed.

PERHAPS the most striking example of an oligarchy is Panama's. There the Veinte Familias (Twenty Families), who are often derisively called the Rabiblancos (White-tailed Birds), have been intermarrying for three generations. Espinosas have married Ariases and Ariases have married De la Guardias. Paredeses have married Vallarinos, Boyds and Galindos. No one, possibly excepting a family matriarch or two, can now disentangle them.

The Rabiblancos constitute less than 1 per cent of Panama's population, but they own half of all the land not owned by the Government. They own the banks, the breweries, the newspapers, the radio and television stations, the sugar mills, the coffee plantations, the insurance companies, the construction industry, the luxury shops for tourists. Many represent U.S. companies that do business in Panama. On every board of directors one finds the same names.

The Panamanian oligarchs not only dominate the economy of the country; they also dominate its politics. Almost all of Panama's presidents have been members of these wealthy families. Nobody else gets a chance to run. One of the candidates for president in the election of 1963 was Arnulfo Arias, a Harvard-educated coffee planter. Among his opponents was Juan de Arco Galindo, a wealthy engineer who was trained at Georgia Institute of Technology. Galindo's running mate was Gilberto Arias, Arnulfo's nephew. A third candidate was Marco Robles, a cousin of the outgoing President, Roberto F. Chiari. A fourth was Miguel J. Moreno Jr. Moreno's wife, the former Graciela Gasteazoro, is the sister-in-law of Raul Arango, who was Robles' running mate.

Not only were all the candidates connected with each other in one way or another; they were related to other members of the oligarchy: to the De la Guardias, the Espinosas, the Vallarinos. No matter which candidate won the election, the group as a whole could not lose.

Much of the wealth of the Rabiblancos comes from real estate. The Espinosa family, for example, long ago acquired extensive holdings in what is now downtown Panama City. When the United States built the Panama Canal, Panama City boomed and the land became valuable—and the Espinosas became rich. The Icazas, the Fábregas and the Obarrios also owe their considerable wealth to real estate.

LEADING FAMILIES: A DIRECTORY

EL SALVADOR: Wealthiest of the groups in Central America, El Salvador's leading families are known as the Catorce Grande, or "Big Fourteen." Most of the millionaire families are of recent vintage, rarely going back more than a generation or so. Family fortunes are based almost entirely on coffee, politics and cotton.

PANAMA: Some two dozen families known as the Rabiblancos (after a Central American bird whose meat is white) or as the Veinte (Twenty) Familias constitute Panama's leading group. Like El Salvador's, most of the wealthy Panamanian families became prominent only a couple of generations ago. Their wealth is largely based on coffee, sugar and real estate.

NICARAGUA: The 20-odd outstanding families have no particular nickname. Many of them have inherited wealth from ancestors who received land grants from the Spanish Crown; others base more recently acquired fortunes on cattle and coffee.

GUATEMALA: Its relatively few wealthy families, also lacking a nickname, base their money on real estate, industry and coffee.

COSTA RICA AND HONDURAS: Neither nation has families of great wealth.

The oligarchs unfortunately have done relatively little to develop Panama. They have started cattle ranches around the towns of David and Chitré, but they have left the rest of the country almost a wilderness. This is not because they invest their money abroad; by and large, unlike many wealthy Latin Americans, they do not. They just see no reason to develop the countryside when there are so many opportunities for profit in Panama City and Colón. The slums of those cities are gold mines for them; they can wrest exorbitant rents from the slum dwellers, who have no place else to live, and they can demand high prices for clothing and food because they dominate the economy. Former President Chiari's Blue Star Dairy supplies most of Panama's milk and dairy products. He can, therefore, charge almost what he chooses. Chiari also has a near stranglehold on sugar production; Panamanians have to pay nearly twice as much for sugar as the people who live in the U.S.-run Canal Zone.

It must be conceded that to develop the jungles of Panama into a profitable agricultural region would be an exceedingly difficult undertaking. None of the oligarchs, however wealthy, could do more than develop a few hundred acres, and the unstable governments of Panama do not have the power to engage in such a mammoth project. It must also be conceded that business monopolies are almost inevitable in a country as small and poor as Panama. The country's economy simply cannot support several competing cement companies or dairies, and mass production, which would reduce costs, is likewise impractical. But it must also be said that the oligarchs have made little effort so to organize the country that steps toward improving its economy and the lot of its people could be taken.

For years the Rabiblancos have cast covetous eyes on the Canal Zone. There is money in the Zone, for not only are the Americans paid wages that are considered fabulous by Panamanian standards, but so are the Panamanians who work there. The oligarchs successfully agitated to have Panamanian citizens barred as of December 31, 1956, from the Zone's U.S. commissaries, where they were buying food and other goods at moderate prices.

Socially, the oligarchic families are divided into three groups: those that came from Old Spain, those that emigrated from Europe and the Middle East, and those with Negro blood. The distinctions are becoming more and more blurred as the families intermarry. Nevertheless, they persist in occasional snide remarks. A family that came from Old Spain may say of a family of newcomers, "They're *de afuera*," that is, "outsiders." The old family considers itself *de adentro*, or "from the inside." A family that claims to have no Negro ancestors may say of another that does, "They have kinky hair."

Intermarriage is not the only reason the distinctions are becoming more and more blurred. The oligarchs are obviously extremely money-conscious; few of the *adentros*, the "oldtimers," have as much wealth as the "outsider" *afueras*. The Maduro family may have Dutch ancestors and the Boyds Irish, the Chiaris Italian and the Eletas Spanish, but they all can buy and sell most of the *adentros*. As for the families with some Negro ancestors, Panamanians have a saying: "Money makes everyone white."

MANY of the Panamanian oligarchs live modestly, in homes that cost between $50,000 and $65,000. Servants are cheap (they are paid an average of $40 a month), so each wealthy family usually has at least a chauffeur, a gardener, a cook, one or two housemaids and a nursemaid. The families send their sons to Harvard, Yale or Georgetown and marry off the girls as quickly as possible. A girl of 20 who has not yet become engaged is considered in danger of becoming an old maid.

The Panamanian oligarchs travel widely in the U.S. and Europe. Abroad, they do splurge, but at home they try to avoid ostentation. The women spend their days playing cards, going to luncheons and doing charity work. The men devote their waking hours to business and politics. Most wealthy Panamanians go through a playboy stage between 15 and 25, but once they settle down, business and politics become almost obsessions with them. They rush off to their offices around 9:30 in the morning and stay there until 9 or 10 at night. Unlike many Latins, the wealthy Panamanians do not go home for lunch; they grab a quick bite around the corner. The siesta is something they have only read about in books.

EL SALVADOR's oligarchs, the Catorce Grande, provide a sharp contrast with the Rabiblancos. Hardly any of them are descended from old families; many are immigrants. Their fortunes are based on coffee, cotton—and politics.

By and large, they are extremely progressive in business. They constantly invest their money in the development of their country. The Catorce Grande also live the lives of men of wealth. They have lavish homes in town and imposing estates in the country. They work in fancy, air-conditioned offices and drive to work in flashy sports cars. The women wear the latest dresses from New York, Paris and Rome.

The country club is the center of social life for El Salvador's wealthy families. All the members of the Catorce Grande love sports: tennis, golf, swimming and horseback riding. The men have a passion for polo. Many of the men also are amateur pilots with airstrips on their plantations to which they fly in their own planes.

One of the wealthiest of the Catorce Grande is Benjamín Sol. Don Benjamín, as he is called, made his fortune, an estimated $25 million, in coffee in the late 1920s when coffee prices rose sky-high. His son Roberto now runs the family estates, while Don Benjamín spends most of his time as counselor of the Salvadoran Embassy in Paris.

Perhaps the most interesting of the Catorce Grande are the De Solas. Don Herbert de Sola came to El Salvador in 1895 from Curaçao, where his family had lived for generations, and opened a small dry-goods store. The store prospered, and by 1905 Don Herbert had accumulated enough money to buy a small soap factory. This, too, prospered. He went into exporting coffee and sugar, started a candle factory and then built another factory, the first of its kind in El Salvador, to manufacture cooking oil, shortening and margarine from cotton seed.

The De Solas are the second-biggest exporters of coffee in the country, and they have vastly expanded their industrial enterprise as well. They own 10 per cent of a soluble-coffee plant (the Rockefellers own 50 per cent) and 20 per cent of a Pillsbury-sponsored flour mill. The De Solas helped to finance and set up a chemical-fertilizer plant, and they also own a sugar mill. The estimated worth of the De Sola complex is 30 million dollars.

The oldest of Don Herbert's sons, Victor, runs the family's coffee and commercial enterprises, while the youngest, Francisco, watches over the manufacturing operations. A third son, Orlando, recently deceased, was a physician; a fourth, Ernesto, is El Salvador's most prominent architect and construction engineer.

Proud of his Dutch citizenship, Don Herbert, who died in 1963, never became a Salvadoran. Nevertheless, he was extremely civic-minded. He established a foundation to grant scholarships to needy students, endowed a medical laboratory and maintained four hospitals for rural workers. He supported the local musical society and the symphony.

His sons are equally civic-minded. Among other things, they have organized a finance company for small business. Victor has argued that helping other men expand the nation's commerce would help all business, including the De Solas', because it would create more wage earners and a bigger market. This kind of advanced thinking was once unique in Central America; it remains, unfortunately, rather rare.

BUT if other members of the Catorce Grande are not as forward-looking as the De Solas, they have nonetheless done a great deal for the Salvadoran economy. El Salvador is a highly developed country by Central American standards. The Catorce Grande use modern farming methods, importing as much fertilizer as the rest of Central America put together. El Salvador has one of the world's highest per acre yields of coffee and is second only to California in per acre yield of cotton. The Catorce Grande have been equally progressive in business.

Until recently, however, the Catorce Grande resisted social change. It took a military dictatorship, which seized power in 1960, to force them to pay their workers a minimum wage of 70 cents a day, to reduce slum rents and to make other reforms necessary for the country to qualify for participation in the Alliance for Progress. Men who own strings of polo ponies sat in hotel bars cursing "this damned outrage." When the dictatorship nationalized El Salvador's main bank, they were apoplectic. They took out ads in the newspapers denouncing the move and bemoaning the fact that El Salvador had lost the distinction of having a privately owned national bank.

One did not find the more progressive De Solas talking like this, however, or those members of the other families who have absorbed some liberal political ideas. And many of the sons of the other families have returned from schools in the U.S. with the idea that Indians and mestizos are human beings, not animals. However, this is still a minority view.

IN Guatemala the oligarchs are not as wealthy as the Rabiblancos and the Catorce Grande, nor as powerful. Guatemala has a middle class, and the wealth is spread more evenly than in Panama and El Salvador; in fact, the aggregate wealth of the middle class is probably as great as that of the oligarchy.

The oligarchs, therefore, do not dominate the economy of Guatemala as they do the economies of Panama and El Salvador. Nor do they dominate the social life. Actually, they are almost indistinguishable from the middle class in appearance and in way of life. They live in slightly bigger houses and drive slightly bigger cars, and their wives wear somewhat better clothes. The wives, however, work side by side with middle-class wives in charitable organizations, and the husbands swim and ride with middle-class business and professional men at the country club.

Wealthiest of all the Guatemalan oligarchs are the Herreras. The Herreras were followers of the dictator Justo Rufino Barrios, who hated the Church and confiscated its land. The Church's loss was the Herreras' gain. They now are the richest landowners in the country, growing coffee and sugar.

Guatemala, like El Salvador, has its progressive families. Among them are the Castillos. In 1886 the brothers Rafael and Mariano Castillo established Guatemala's first brewery. The business flourished and Cerveceria Centroamericana is now a $20 million enterprise. The brewery is located on Finca Zapote at Guatemala City's northern edge and resembles a miniature town, complete with church and schoolhouse. It employs some 500 workers, all of whom are union members. Cerveceria's union contract is considered among the most enlightened in Central America. The fringe benefits include medical and dental care for all workers and their families, about 3,000 people in all. Dr. Mariano Castillo Samayoa is the chief physician; his cousin, Raul Castillo, runs the dental clinic.

Cerveceria maintains a small loan fund from which workers may borrow without interest. All workers are given a free bottle of beer at lunchtime and three more bottles to take home to their families after work. Since the union has a bylaw denying full status to illiterates, the company runs a school for employees who cannot read and write. The brewery recently built a school in the Jocotales section of Guatemala City at a cost of $100,000. Classes are free, and the 300 children who attend also get a free lunch.

While the brewery flourished, the Castillo family flourished, too. The third generation now numbers about 200. Since Guatemalan law provides that all the sons must share equally in a father's estate, there are few wealthy Castillos. Some, in fact, are rich only in social standing. José Mariano Arzú Castillo, who runs the brewery's public relations department, is exaggerating only slightly when he says, "The time will come when, if the business keeps being divided among the family, we'll end up with one bottle of beer each."

IN Nicaragua the position of the oligarchic families is a peculiar one. They do not form a well-knit group because they are split between those who support the Somozas and those who detest them. Many of Nicaragua's oligarchs—the Pellas family, for example—are outspoken in their opposition to Tachito Somoza and his brother Luis.

Luis uses this opposition to justify his failure to push through really progressive measures. Once, for example, in discussing tax reform, he told a correspondent from the United States: "You say that my brother and I are dictators. If Tachito and I ever came out for higher taxes, you'd see what kind of dictators we are. The big landowners would rise up and throw us out."

This was pure sophistry, of course. Luis and Tachito oppose higher taxes because they themselves would have to pay them, not because they fear an uprising of the other big landowners. The Somozas are notorious for their ability to avoid taxes. Once they gave some of their land to a charity. They said, correctly, that it was worth $1.5 million. For years they had valued the property for tax purposes at $7,000.

Nevertheless, the fact remains that most of the Nicaraguan oligarchs are even more conservative than Luis and Tachito. Many are the descendants of Spanish hidalgos who received land grants from the Crown. They are a pleasant group, however, hospitable and completely lacking in snobbishness. Despite their political conservatism, they think nothing of putting on a pair of blue jeans and dropping into a neighborhood cantina to drink and chat with the workingmen and peasants.

THE Nicaraguan oligarchs do not really live on the estates they inherited from their ancestors. They live in town in homes very much like those one finds in well-to-do U.S. suburbs, complete with swimming pools. However, they are not absentee landlords. They visit their estates frequently and vacation on them. But they take life easy. Unlike the Panamanians, they do not believe in working hard; unlike the Salvadorans, they are content with what they have. In fact, the Nicaraguan oligarchs like the status quo and they hope to maintain it.

Among the more liberal of the Nicaraguan oligarchic families are the Sacasas, but they would hardly be considered liberal anywhere else. Members of the younger generation of the Sacasas believe in what they call "gradualism." This means change—but a little at a time in order to avoid any disruption of the economy or the social system. In this frame of mind, the Sacasas have sponsored moderate social reforms in recent years, such as paid vacations for workers, social security and a minimum wage. And unlike many of their fellow oligarchs, they are scrupulous about paying the minimum wage—six cordobas, approximately 87 cents a day—plus a meal of rice, beans and boiled plantains.

For a family like the Sacasas to advocate even limited reforms is, in a way, remarkable. Their wealth, an estimated five million dollars in cattle, coffee, real estate and securities, has come down through generations. And for generations they have been identified with the Government and the Church. It was a Sacasa who brought the Nuns of the Assumption to Nicaragua in the early 1890s, and the family still supports the order. Sacasas are everywhere in the Army, the diplomatic corps and the civil service. A Sacasa is the Nicaraguan Ambassador to Washington. To other members of the oligarchy with similar backgrounds, change is simply unthinkable. The Sacasas at least recognize its inevitability.

At that, the Nicaraguan landowners are liberals compared with their Honduran counterparts. In Honduras the landowners seem still to live not even in the 19th Century, but in the 17th. They are backward economically as well as politically. Only two or three of them are wealthy even by Guatemalan standards; the rest are merely well-to-do. They are content. They like things just as they are.

A U.S. businessman in Tegucigalpa once explained why. "I've been trying for two years to get permission to build a lumber mill," he said. "I can't. All the landowners in the neighborhood ganged up against me. I spoke to one; I asked him why. He said, 'We don't want industry anywhere near us. Factories pay higher wages than we can. They draw workers off the land. They make those who remain on the land restless. Union organizers come in; Communists come in. We're doing all right. Leave us alone.' "

THE Honduran landowner was no fool. He recognized one thing: the oligarchies can remain in power only so long as Central America remains primarily agricultural and most of the land remains concentrated in a few hands. Only the development of industry, with its attendant increase in literacy and in the power of the workingman and of unions, can break the grip of the big landowners.

Industry, when it comes, will force literacy on Central America, unions will follow industry and wages will rise. If higher wages at first cut into the profits of the industrialists, the increased prosperity of the workers will eventually broaden the industrialists' markets. A worker who makes $1.50 a day, as many of Panama's agricultural workers do, can hardly be called a market. But eventually industry will grow and with it a skilled working class and a middle class. Unions and a middle class will give Central America what it does not have yet: a countervailing political force. As long as most of Central America lives on the land, as long as Central America (outside Panama and Costa Rica) is 64 per cent illiterate, no such countervailing political force can arise. Democratic government under these circumstances cannot be anything but a caricature. There cannot at present be such a thing as secret voting since the average farm worker cannot read the ballot and must have it read to him by the landowner's agent. If he votes against the landowner's wishes, he may be thrown out of his house and lose his job.

The Honduran landowner cited above is not alone in realizing that change, and especially industrialization, is his enemy. Most of the oligarchs do. They know that a countervailing political force will weaken their grip on the Government. Someday the peasants will become informed and independent voters and will demand a meaningful tax system. The oligarchs much prefer a tax system like Nicaragua's, where the Somozas can evaluate property for tax purposes at $7,000 when the real worth is $1.5 million.

IF the oligarchs do not build roads or develop the remote regions of Panama, Honduras and Guatemala that now are virtually uninhabited, it is again not merely because roads cost money. If they were sure that they could control the land themselves, the oligarchs would build the roads and clear the jungle. What they fear is that a clamor would arise from the landless for the Government to divide the land. This would create a class of independent small farmers like Costa Rica's. Peons are easier to handle.

The oligarchs are not stupid men by any means. Many are highly intelligent and well educated, with beautiful, charming wives. Sometimes, however, they must be saved from themselves, as the military saved the Catorce Grande in El Salvador by instituting reforms. In Panama, the United States may have to save them, for the oligarchs may not always be able to control the mob. Someday the mob may realize who the real enemy is—that it is not the Zonians or the United States, but the men who pay them 40 cents an hour while charging them 30 cents for a quart of milk and 60 cents for a dozen eggs.

Small Aristocracies of Wealth and Power

In most of Central America, there are basically two classes of people—those who own almost everything and those who own virtually nothing. For centuries the families of wealth used their power absolutely, almost in the haughty manner of the conquistadors who originally established the two-class social pattern. Yet while the ways of wealth—expensive sports, isolated estates, exclusive clubs—endure, and are pursued and enjoyed as of old, the U.S.- and European-educated sons and daughters of the wealthy have become not only well traveled and well read, like their forefathers, but also, unlike them, believers in progressive concepts of social justice.

VACATION RETREATS, modern houses with generous swimming pools cling to tiny islands in Lake Nicaragua. The pools serve a practical purpose: the lake contains fresh-water sharks.

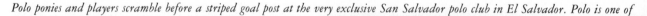

Polo ponies and players scramble before a striped goal post at the very exclusive San Salvador polo club in El Salvador. Polo is one of

CARNIVAL PARTY for children of the Guatemala City elite fills the colonial-style Club Guatemala. Some of the children are dressed in costume for the affair, a part of the club's and the city's pre-Lenten festivities. Guatemala has a small but influential middle class, and the rich are not so dominant a social force as they are in most of the Central American countries.

the most popular diversions of the wealthy upper class in El Salvador. The club's team captured the Central American trophy in 1963.

LEADING BUSINESSMEN enlarge their fortunes as they experiment with new techniques

COTTON PLANTER, Juan Wright of El Salvador *(above)* inspects a section of the cotton gin on his property. Wright began growing cotton a decade ago and has made his fortune with it.

SUGAR PRODUCER, Alfredo Pellas surveys a mill *(left)* on his Nicaraguan plantation. A progressive employer, Pellas allots 10 per cent of his profits for division among his 4,000 workers.

COFFEE GROWERS, the Stahl brothers of Guatemala, Gustavo *(opposite, in doorway)* and Rodolfo *(center)*, sample blends with an employee. They export most of their coffee to Europe.

GUATEMALAN MILLIONAIRE, Rafael Herrera oversees his large sugar and coffee plantations from his Guatemala City office. The Herrera family fortune dates back to the 19th Century.

NICARAGUAN BANKER, Dr. Francisco Lainez works in the Managua office of the country's Central Bank, of which he is president. The bank regulates the national credit system.

YOUNG MATRONS increasingly perform volunteer charity work among the children of the poor

ENCOURAGING A CHILD to read Braille, Mrs. Elisa Molina de Stahl, Guatemala's Secretary of Social Welfare and wife of coffee planter Rodolfo Stahl, works in a school for the blind.

TALKING WITH A NURSE, Mrs. Juan Wright visits a school for blind and deaf children in San Salvador *(right)*. Mrs. Wright also helps manage day-care centers for poor children.

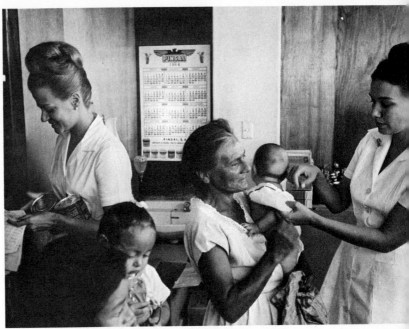

DISTRIBUTING MILK, two young San Salvador women help care for patients in the modern, eight-million-dollar Bloom Hospital, where milk is given free to babies from poor families.

EXAMINING A BABY, Mrs. Coya Paz de Talavera, whose husband is a San Salvador radio broadcaster, gives assistance to the staff in the outpatient department of the new Bloom Hospital.

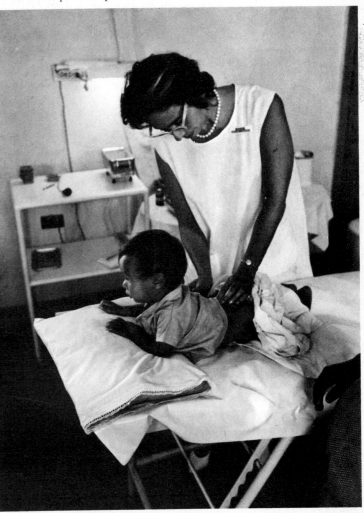

President Francisco José Orlich of Costa Rica addresses spectators at a charity fair in San José in 1964. Costa Rica's regularly held, free

elections make the country the most democratic in Central America.

8

Democrats and Dictators

THE late President Anastasio "Tacho" Somoza of Nicaragua once visited the Dominican Republic with his wife. The story goes that the visit was a short one, for Tacho apparently took an instant dislike to Rafael Trujillo, the self-styled *Benefactor* of the Dominican Republic. At dinner in the presidential palace in Managua a few days later, a distinguished visitor from the U.S. started twitting Somoza. "Why did you cut the visit short?" he asked. Somoza merely shrugged. The guest kept after him, but the answer finally came from Mrs. Somoza. "Why, do you know," she cried indignantly, "that man Trujillo is a dictator!"

Tacho Somoza, who ruled Nicaragua from 1936, when he drove his own uncle, Juan Bautista Sacasa, from the presidency, until 1956, when an ungrateful subject shot him to death, never really considered himself a dictator. He thought of himself, instead, as a father, strict but fair, whose children included the entire population of the country.

"I would like nothing better than to give [the Nicaraguan people] the same kind of freedom as that of the United States," he once said. And then he added that, unfortunately, giving people freedom was like bringing up a baby. "First you give it milk by drops, then more and more, then a little piece of pig, and finally it can eat everything. . . ." Clearly, freedom could be fed to Nicaragua only a spoonful at a time. But actually, as dictators go, Tacho was a tower of benevolence. He rarely killed his opponents; he preferred to put them in jail until they repented their sins. Occasionally, to help them repent more quickly, his police used a little torture, but still it could not be said that Tacho was a fiend.

Tacho Somoza had a style all his own; contemporary Central American political leaders are required to present a more civilized veneer. They live in a new world, one in which they have to cope with a business and professional class that, if not large or powerful, nevertheless can be highly vocal; they have to cope also with Communists and Castroites.

SOMOZA'S sons are an example of the new breed. After the old man's death, the older son, Luis, took over the presidency, while the younger, "Tachito," assumed command of the National Guard. Tachito Somoza is the muscle behind Nicaragua's new-style dictatorship. A graduate of West Point (Class of 1946), pudgy and tight-lipped, he is a no-nonsense soldier who has made his National Guard into the best-disciplined, best-trained and most efficient army in Central America.

It is a lean force, totaling some 5,000 officers and men. About 1,000 of them are members of an elite striking force known as the "General Somoza Combat Battalion"; the rest perform guard, police and support duties.

Officers spend three years at the military academy in Managua, which was reorganized by Tachito, and there they receive a junior-college education as well as a military one. Then they spend a year abroad, usually at Fort Gulick in the Canal Zone. Their salaries are not high, ranging from $100 a month for second lieutenants to $300 for colonels. However, the housing is better than adequate and the commissaries sell such luxuries (for Central America) as radios and refrigerators at cost. Even more important, perhaps, officers and their wives are not searched when they go through customs on return from foreign trips. Tachito does not frown upon a tolerable amount of smuggling.

The enlisted men receive food, medical care, four uniforms a year and $20 a month, and for a Nicaraguan peasant, that is a fortune. Their training, however, is tough and constant. Tachito orders his men to go on the firing range at least twice a year, and on maneuvers at least once a year. He boasts that nine tenths of his men are sharpshooters.

TACHITO does not tolerate politics in the Guard, and there are none. Officers, noncommissioned officers and troops alike have demonstrated devotion to the Somoza cause again and again. Since Tachito took over the Guard, there have been no fewer than 75 rebellions and border crossings by armed exiles. The Guard has gone into action to put them down almost by reflex. No Guard unit has ever defected.

While Tachito provides the Somoza muscle, his brother Luis provides the voice. Luis is very much like his father, a jovial man who takes a tolerant view of critics of the Somoza family; he cracks down on them only when he thinks it is absolutely necessary, and even then punishment is rarely severe.

Luis is the kind of person who tells stories like this: One day he ran into General Emiliano Chamorro Vargas, a Conservative leader and an old enemy of the family who was once exiled for plotting the assassination of Tacho Somoza. "I met the old man," Luis will say, "and he asks me, 'How many kids do you now have?' I tell him six boys and a girl. Then he says, 'Good God! Will we never finish with you Somozas?' "

After Luis and Tachito took over the country, they noticeably softened the dictatorship. Luis permitted moderate freedom of speech and of the press. He even permitted moderate freedom of assembly, but he absolutely forbade radio broadcasts likely to "undermine public order." The reason for his differentiation between the press and the radio was perfectly understandable. Only 35 per cent of the Nicaraguan people can read, and most of these naturally take a skeptical view of the Somozas anyway. What concerned Luis was the 65 per cent who cannot read but who are within hearing distance of a radio.

By 1958, Luis was talking like a democrat—and in colloquial American, too, for, like his brother, he went to school in the U.S. (he studied agronomy at the University of California and did postgraduate work at Louisiana State and the University of Maryland). He actually suggested that Congress pass a law barring him from succeeding himself when his official six-year term was up.

No one in Nicaragua took him seriously, of course. Everyone felt that the suggestion was intended solely to curry favor with Washington. When President Kennedy announced his Alliance for Progress, Luis was among the first to applaud. With Alliance money he built low-cost housing and schools and set up rural credit agencies.

He outdid himself. He pushed a law through Congress that not only barred him from running for reelection but also barred any member of his immediate family (meaning his brother Tachito) from succeeding him. In addition, a law was passed permitting any party with 15,000 members to put up a candidate for president. And it cut the presidential term from six years to four.

The election was set for February 1963. The Somoza candidate was René Schick, a lawyer by profession and a former Foreign Minister. His principal opponent was Dr. Fernando Agüero, an oculist. The candidate of the Traditionalist Conservative Party, Dr. Agüero had once led an unsuccessful attempt to oust the Somozas. There was a third candidate, Diego Manuel Chamorro, leader of a pro-Somoza splinter of the Conservative Party.

AGUERO refused to believe that the Somozas intended to hold a fair election, and he called for supervision by the United Nations or the Organization of American States. Luis scornfully rejected the demand, suggesting that it was an aspersion on the honor of the Nicaraguan Government. Then, Luis gave Agüero good reason to anticipate a rigged election. He arranged to have four of the five seats on the Supreme Electoral Tribunal, which supervises Nicaragua's elections, filled by his men. In a rage, Agüero quit the campaign. "We won't be a party to a fraud rigged by the Somozas," he said.

A week before the election, Luis asked the O.A.S. to suggest the names of three men who might come, at the Nicaraguan Government's expense, to observe the balloting. There was little point in their coming.

With Agüero out, Schick won in a walk. A somewhat colorless man with a reputation for honesty and a gift for platitudes, he went on the radio to pledge: "I will never be a puppet of anyone. . . . I have a high sense of personal dignity. . . . God will help me not to be a puppet President. . . ."

AT the same time, Schick renamed Tachito commander of the Guard. And this, of course, made a mockery of his pledge. For with Tachito controlling the military power of Nicaragua and Luis controlling a major part of the economy, Schick is hardly in a position to act independently of the Somoza family. He has as much freedom of action as Luis and Tachito choose to give him.

In 1967, there will be another presidential election. Then, both Luis and Tachito will be eligible to run. Luis says he would "hate to . . . but, if things go bad, I may have to." His brother says: "Every Nicaraguan would some day like to become president. I'm no exception."

In a highly uncertain world, this much is about as certain as anything can be: no matter how much Schick may voice his independence during his Administration, the Somozas will continue to rule Nicaragua. And whether Schick is succeeded by Luis or Tachito, the Somozas still will rule. The answer to Chamorro Vargas' question, "Will we never finish with you Somozas?" is, No, not in the foreseeable future.

It is far less easy to make predictions about Guatemala. Since 1944, Guatemala has run through nearly a dozen different dictatorships of varying political ideologies. Following the overthrow in 1944 of Jorge Ubico, the dictator with a passion for cleanliness (see Chapter 4), a presidential election brought Juan José Arévalo to power in 1945. Arévalo called himself a "spiritual Socialist." As President he was, in fact, a democrat with Marxist leanings; he was outspokenly anti-American, but neither pro- nor anti-Communist. He apparently regarded Communism as an innocuous doctrine, but perhaps something of a political danger. Yet he neither pampered nor suppressed the Communists.

Arévalo walked a tightrope because control of the Army, the real power in Guatemala, was almost evenly divided between two Guatemalan colonels,

Jacobo Arenz Guzmán and Francisco Javier Arana.

In July 1949, Arana was assassinated. It was generally assumed in Guatemala that Arbenz had arranged the killing. As President, Arévalo made no attempt to find out the truth of the charges, and for the Guatemalan Army officer corps, that was the final straw. It became his enemy. But with Arana dead, Arbenz had no real opposition when he ran for the presidency in December 1950, and he was elected by an overwhelming margin.

ARBENZ devoted himself to social reform, particularly to land reform. He confiscated the unused land of the wealthy, as well as huge tracts owned by the United Fruit Company, and distributed the seized land among the peasants. To carry out his program, however, he filled his Government with Communists, and he also made it clear where his international sympathies lay; during the Korean War, for example, he allowed propaganda to circulate accusing the U.S. of biological warfare. Moreover, he further infuriated the officer corps by proposing the establishment of a workers' militia which would be independent of Army control. With the acquiescence of the Army and the aid of the United States, he was ousted in 1954 (see Chapter 5) and his place taken by Carlos Castillo Armas, an Army colonel.

Having suffered through an old-fashioned dictatorship under Ubico, a Liberal-Leftist Government under Arévalo and a pro-Communist Government under Arbenz, Guatemala then went through a violently anti-Communist phase. Everybody was a "Communist," except for the anointed few, and even some of them were suspect.

Castillo Armas himself was a decent man and an honest one. Although he ran a dictatorship, he continued some of the social reforms started by his predecessors. He proceeded with agrarian reform, for example, albeit at a much slower pace. But the men around Castillo Armas were rapacious; they were by no means reluctant to use their positions to enrich themselves. Anyone who dared to object was instantly labeled a Communist.

In July 1957, Castillo Armas was assassinated. His killer committed suicide without revealing the names of his associates—if any. The Government naturally blamed the Communists, but it never produced any

evidence to support the charge, and no one was ever arrested for the crime. Months of turmoil followed. Finally, in March 1958, Miguel Ydígoras Fuentes became President.

Only a novelist, perhaps only a Balzac, could do justice to Ydígoras. The man is what the French call "an original."

Ydígoras took over a country fragmented politically, and he managed to govern it for five years by playing each faction against the others. It was a brilliant performance but also a bewildering one. Later, *El Imparcial*, Guatemala City's leading newspaper, was to say: "We Guatemalans were living like spectators at a ping-pong game, looking from side to side as the Ydígoras Government switched position from day to day, capricious and unstable."

Ydígoras allowed the United States to train Cuban exiles on Guatemalan soil for the abortive landing in the Bay of Pigs. He also permitted Communist leaders who had been exiled by Castillo Armas to return to Guatemala. "I like them where I can see them," he explained. "I tell all these Reds: 'There are two doors in Guatemala. One door leads to freedom; the other is the door of your cell in jail. Take your choice. I'll let you talk but, start trouble, you're going to jail.'"

HE brought Guatemalan-Mexican relations to one of their lowest points by ordering his air force to attack Mexican shrimp boats for allegedly poaching in Guatemalan waters. He threatened economic warfare against Britain over British Honduras, which Guatemala claims, and once threatened to invade the territory. He said the United States had promised to support his claim as part of the bargain under which he permitted the U.S. to use Guatemala as a training base for the Cuban exiles. This the Department of State vehemently denied.

Ydígoras concerned himself with domestic matters as well. Once he issued an order for the dismissal of Government officials who had mistresses. No official could afford a mistress on a Government salary, Ydígoras explained. Having a mistress, therefore, was prima-facie evidence that a Cabinet member was taking graft.

In point of fact, Ydígoras' worries were probably well founded. Accusations of corruption were heard frequently during his Administration. Several U.S. businessmen complained bitterly to the U.S. Ambassador about kickbacks and graft. Whether or not the charges were true, Ydígoras himself probably did not share in the graft. His salary was $12,000 a month, and in addition he received special tax-free allowances which in one year amounted to $1.8 million.

Ordinarily Guatemalans, like Latin Americans generally, accept graft as a fact of life. But the reports of widespread corruption in the Government provided ample ammunition to Ydígoras' enemies. There were frequent demonstrations. In January 1962, Ydígoras attempted to quiet the clamor by appearing on national television. Pointing to members of his Cabinet seated behind him, he asked the TV audience: "Now, do these men have crooked, dishonest faces?" And he answered the question himself —in the negative.

Nothing so became him as the manner of his leaving office. Arévalo was in exile in Mexico, hoping to return to Guatemala and run for the presidency. Ydígoras announced that he would arrest Arévalo if he returned. Nevertheless, Arévalo managed to enter the country and even to hold a press conference on Guatemalan soil. Fearing Arévalo's return to power, the Army, under Colonel Enrique Peralta Azurdia, thereupon seized control of the Government "for the good of the nation." Ydígoras was arrested on March 30, 1963, and left for Nicaragua. There he declared that the coup d'état had actually been for the good of Guatemala and for that of "the rest of Central America." Later, when accusations were made that he had engineered his own overthrow, he started attacking Peralta.

Peralta and a small clutch of Army officers and civilians rapidly established control over Guatemala. The talk of graft largely disappeared after Peralta

> ## POLITICAL TURMOIL: AN EXAMPLE
>
> The often reported political instability of Central America is by no means a recent phenomenon. To cite an example, Honduras alone had no fewer than 30 presidents between 1839, the year it became an independent nation, and 1963, when a junta ousted President Ramón Villeda Morales. Its first President, Francisco Ferrera, served two terms. But of the next five presidents, one resigned, two were overthrown, one died in office and another was assassinated. One leader, José María Medina, first became a provisional President in June 1863, then surrendered the office in December, only to return to it in February 1864 as an elected President. He again became a provisional President in 1865, then was elected again in 1866 and 1870. Tiburcio Carías Andino held the office longer than anyone else, from 1933 to 1949, when he turned it over to Juan Manuel Gálvez. Gálvez left the country in 1954 for medical attention, and was succeeded by his Vice President, Julio Lozano Díaz. Ousted in 1956, Lozano Díaz was eventually succeeded by Villeda Morales.

launched a program of reform that he called "Operation Honesty," which proved remarkably effective. Signs everywhere in Government offices advised the public to denounce any effort at extracting money by a Government employee. While the practices of padding contracts and bribing officials, especially on lower levels where policing is difficult, did not entirely disappear, both foreign and domestic businessmen agreed that the Peralta Administration was perhaps the most honest in the country's history.

Beyond that, Peralta's Government has been administratively efficient and relatively relaxed politically. Government workers are paid on schedule, and debts to Government suppliers are being liquidated. The Government allows newspapers to print, and people to say, pretty much what they want —as long as they do not become too outspokenly critical. There are very few opponents of the regime in jail; the Government deported most of the people it did not like. Moreover, when a Constituent Assembly appointed after Peralta's accession to revise the Constitution has completed its work, national elections will be held. No date for them had been scheduled as of 1964, but Guatemala had been given peace and quiet after years of turmoil; for most Guatemalans that was a vast improvement on the past.

Honduras is ruled by the military, too, but the situation there is quite different. The country is seething, as usual. The military coup that ousted President Ramón Villeda Morales in October 1963 and made Colonel Osvaldo López dictator was the 136th revolution in the 142 years that Honduras has been independent from Spain. It almost certainly will not be the last.

A pediatrician by profession, and the author of several respected works in his field, Villeda Morales was a mild-mannered reformer who strove for nearly six years to bring Honduras into the 20th Century. Using Alliance for Progress money, he built roads and schools. He also launched a modest agrarian-reform program, and he did what he could to attract foreign investment. The big landowners, however, did not find him to their liking, and they fought the reforms he proposed. The landowners, moreover, found allies in the Army, and in Honduras the Army is a semiautonomous organization. It must ask Congress for money, but that is the only control the Government has over it.

To weaken the power of the Army, Villeda Morales created a 2,500-man civil guard that in effect functioned as a private army. Then he made it clear that he would have the civil guard supervise the election of his successor.

That was more than the Army could take. Supervising elections had always been the Army's privilege, one that enabled it to juggle the results. The Army knew that Modesto Rodas Alvarado, president of the Honduran Congress and a political ally of Villeda Morales, unquestionably would be the next President unless it retained its supervising privilege. And Rodas Alvarado had promised to curtail the Army's power even more.

TEN days before the election, the Army struck. As fighter planes swooped low over Tegucigalpa, troops surrounded the presidential palace. After four hours the civil guard surrendered. The Army estimated the casualties at fewer than 100 dead; other estimates ran as high as 1,000. The remnants of the guard were disbanded and Villeda Morales was sent into exile.

Colonel Osvaldo López Arellano, leader of the coup, has talked of restoring constitutional government. Meanwhile, he is making mild efforts at reform, but Honduras has a long road to travel before it emerges from the 19th Century.

In El Salvador, on the other hand, the Army has restored constitutional government, but the President of El Salvador, Julio Adalberto Rivera, is a former Army colonel. Since 1931, every President of El Salvador has been a former Army officer.

One must go back to 1956 to understand how Rivera became President. The election that year was as usual dominated by the Army; the military's man, Lieutenant Colonel José María Lemus, was the only candidate still active in the campaign by election day. The Army announced that a modest 93 per cent of the ballots had been cast for him.

Lemus turned out to be a reasonably good President, but his election had so obviously been rigged that a clamor arose to change the election laws. Lemus did put through a change, but it failed to satisfy his opposition, which he characterized as "a hybrid of Communists and reactionaries."

IN October 1960, after a series of violent riots in the streets, a junta overthrew Lemus and drove him into exile. The leader of the junta was Colonel César Yáñes Urías. Two of the other five members also were Army officers. Another was a physician; two were lawyers. They said they had no concern except to hold a fair election, and they declared themselves out of the running. Social issues could wait until after the election.

Soon there were nine parties in the field, all eager to enter candidates in the promised election. One, a group known as PRAM, from the initial letters of its official name, Partido Revolucionario Abril y Mayo, was composed of students, intellectuals and workers. Pro-Castro, it promised El Salvador a social and economic revolution as sweeping as Cuba's. Another group, known as PSD (Partido Social Demócrata), also was leftist, but more vaguely so.

The Junta de Gobierno, or Governing Junta, arranged for delegates from all nine parties to meet with representatives of the legal profession to draw up a new electoral law. Two days later a rival Army-civilian group known as the Directorio Cívica Militar ousted the Junta and took over the Government. "The armed forces, as well as the widest and most honorable sectors of public opinion," declared a statement issued by the Directorio, "saw with misgiving and fear the growing influence of Communism and of persons and political cliques apparently determined to bring about a climate of unrest, agitation and disorder."

Colonel Adalberto Rivera, who emerged as leader of the Directorio, honestly believed that the Junta had been letting El Salvador drift into Communism, not only because it tolerated PRAM and PSD but also because it avoided grappling with social issues. As Rivera saw it, Communism was inevitable if reforms were not made. The other members of the Directorio felt the same way, and so did the men they elevated to public office.

Rivera was particularly anxious to help the Salvadorean lower classes. Most of the officers in the Army had come from the working class. Many, in fact, were born in the slums of San Salvador and shared his feelings.

By his reforms—an increase in the minimum wage, a cut in tenement rents, the transfer of the Central Reserve Bank from private to Government control—Rivera made himself overwhelmingly popular in the country. When the Directorio held elections in 1961, Rivera's newly formed National Conciliation Party won all 54 of the seats in the Assembly.

As President—an office to which he was elected in 1962—Rivera has been as reform-minded as he was as leader of the Directorio. One of his most effective reforms has been the nationalization of the Central Reserve Bank. By controlling the Bank, the Catorce Grande had controlled the credit system of the country. Small businessmen complained that they could not borrow money to expand; the big families kept the credit system for themselves. In June 1961, the Bank ordered that profits from exports would have to be banked in El Salvador rather than in the U.S., as had previously been the practice. The move made increasing amounts of development capital available to small businessmen.

TODAY El Salvador is enjoying a boom. Foreign capital is entering the country; new factories are springing up. Although the members of the Catorce vehemently opposed the nationalization of the Bank, they have learned to live with the new order of things. They have learned, also, to live with Rivera and even to like him.

Unlike the other Central American republics, Costa Rica has no official army. Its Civil Guard is completely removed from politics; on election days the troops are confined to barracks. The Guard serves strictly as a police force; the guardsmen are like state troopers in the United States.

Ever since José "Pepe" Figueres carried out a revolution in 1948 after the Costa Rican Congress had annulled Otilio Ulate's election as President, the country has been relatively placid politcally. After a brief interlude, Ulate took office in November 1949. He now leads the National Union party, which is basically conservative. Figueres, founder of the liberal Party of National Liberation, followed Ulate into the presidency in 1953 and became the hardest-working President in the history of Costa Rica. He improved the nation's contract with the United Fruit Company, set up a National Institute of Housing and City Planning, doubled top-bracket tax rates and raised minimum wages. The political pendulum swung the other way in the election of 1958, which brought Mario Echandi Jiménez, the candidate of the National Union party, to the presidency. A highly affable man, Echandi was considered by many to be lacking in initiative, and again there was a political reversal: Francisco José Orlich, of the Party of National Liberation, was elected in 1962.

ALL of these Costa Rican elections were completely honest. They took place without disturbances. Costa Ricans accept election results exactly as North Americans do: the decision of the ballot box is final. Unless there is a disastrous drop in commodity prices, one that wrecks the economy, the odds are that Costa Rica in the future will proceed on its democratic course.

There is simply no way of predicting what may happen in Panama. In general, elections have been a private matter among the great Panamanian families known as the Rabiblancos; the people have been given a choice of voting for this member of the Rabiblancos or that one. And for that reason, the elections have been peaceful, if not necessarily honest. Only one president of Panama has ever been assassinated. Nevertheless, there is a sizable, violently anti-American group in the country. Moreover, some Panamanians are oriented to the policies of Fidel Castro. Thelma King, a member of the Panamanian National Assembly who frequently visits Cuba to express her admiration for the Castro revolution, has called for a similar revolution in Panama.

Whether or not the Fidelistas attempt a revolution, Panama remains in danger of social upheaval from one quarter or another. In an unsettled region, it remains one of the most unsettled of nations.

DYNASTIC HEAD, Anastasio "Tacho" Somoza ruled Nicaragua from 1937 until his assassination in 1956. Somoza once challenged a neighboring president to a duel to settle a feud.

DYNASTIC HEIR, Luis Somoza *(above, at head of table)* was made President after his father's death. During his term of office, which ended in 1963, he launched several modest reforms.

FAMILY STRONGMAN, General Anastasio "Tachito" Somoza Jr. *(below)* exercises rigid control over the powerful National Guard. A West Point graduate, he holds presidential ambitions.

BRONZE HORSEMAN, a statue of Tacho Somoza, adorns the dictator's tomb in Managua. The plaque on the base states that the statue was a gift to Somoza from the Nicaraguan people.

A Frequently Stated Loyalty to Democracy

The proclaimed devotion of almost every national leader to the theory of democracy is one of the most striking aspects of Central American politics. But only Costa Rica, with a Government that has established a broad-scale system of public education, consistently puts theory into practice. Elsewhere in the region, political leaders—even those who are genuine reformers—tend to come to government office by methods that could scarcely be characterized as democratic, and many of them manage to maintain themselves in power by consistently exploiting the economic and social frustrations of their citizens.

POWERFUL LEADERS exercise tight control over their countries, but seldom hold office for long

JUNTA HEAD, Colonel Julio Adalberto Rivera overthrew El Salvador's Government in 1961. After winning an unopposed race for President in 1962, he built schools and raised wages.

HAND-PICKED CANDIDATE, René Schick of Nicaragua *(above, left)* confers with his Minister of Economy. He was elected President in 1963 with the backing of the Somoza family.

AUSTERE REVOLUTIONARY, Colonel Enrique Peralta took control of the Guatemalan Government in 1963 to prevent the possible election of popular leftist leader Juan José Arévalo.

VICTORIOUS CAMPAIGNER, Marco A. Robles *(opposite)* was elected President of Panama in 1964. The opposition candidate, ex-President Arnulfo Arias, claimed the election was fixed.

ARMY CHIEF, Colonel Osvaldo López Arellano *(at right, with his wife)* ousted the Honduran Government in 1963. Only two elected Honduran presidents have completed their terms.

BROAD-SCALE EDUCATION in
Costa Rica gives the country
a sound basis for a stable democracy

STUDENT TEACHERS take notes (*above*) in a School of Education class at the University of Costa Rica in San José. Annual tuition is $30, a sum which many poorer persons can afford.

SPACE-AGE BOTANIST, Dr. Carl C. Moh studies plants that have been subjected to radiation in a lab of the Inter-American Institute of Agricultural Sciences in the city of Turrialba.

ATTENTIVE FRESHMEN listen *(below)* to an instructor in a crowded lecture hall at the University. The country's education program still suffers from a shortage of classrooms.

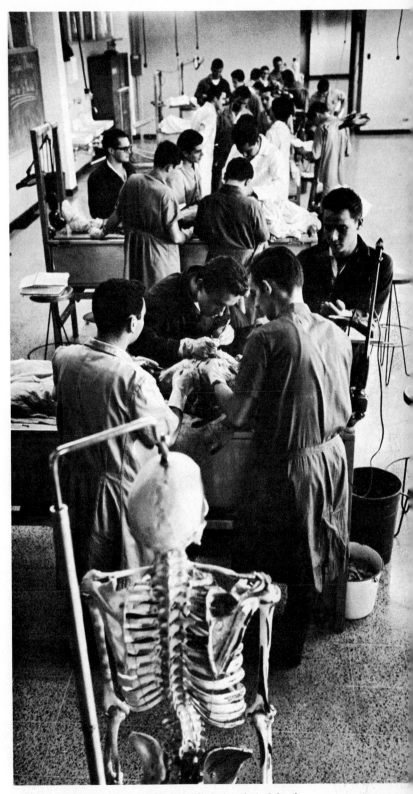

FUTURE DOCTORS dissect cadavers in the university's School of Medicine. The school is endeavoring to supply the needs of a country that has only one physician for each 2,800 persons.

RIOTS protesting U.S. control of the Canal Zone broke out in Panama in 1964

STANDING READY, U.S. soldiers in gas masks *(above)* prepare to repel rioters at the Canal Zone's border. In the background is one of the Panama City slums which stand in sight of the well-kept homes of U.S. citizens living in the Zone.

SHOUTING SLOGANS, Panamanians *(opposite)* surge by the gutted Pan American Airways building in Panama City. The rioting, which lasted nearly a week, erupted after rumors that U.S. high-school students in the Zone had trampled Panama's flag.

RAISING HIS FLAG, a Panamanian secures it to a lamppost *(right)* in the Zone. With an election pending, the country's leaders used the outbreak as an excuse for demanding revision of the treaty by which the U.S. exercises sovereignty in the Zone.

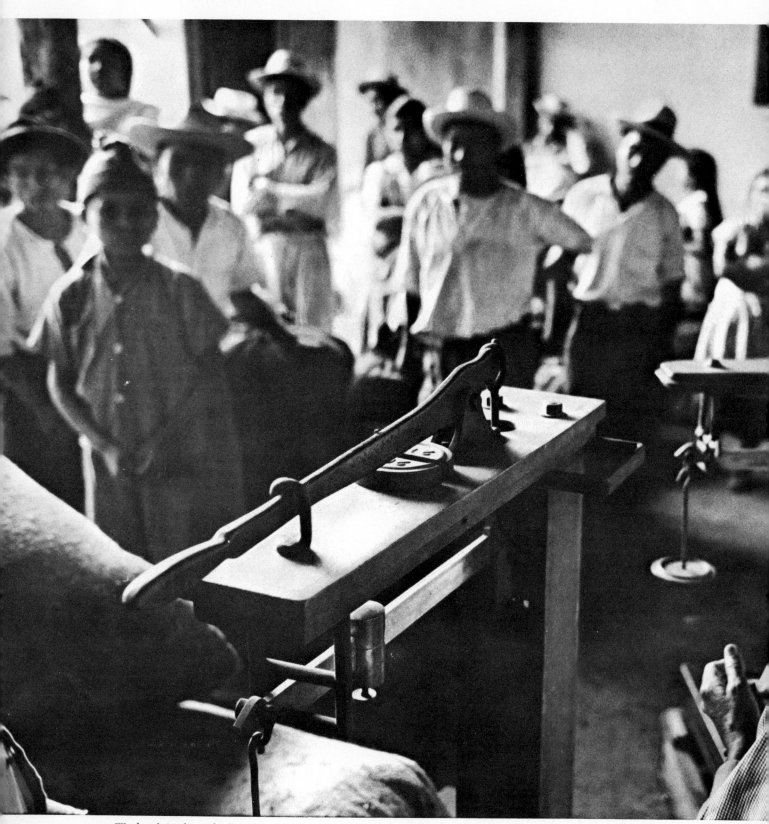

Workers bring bags of coffee to be weighed on a plantation near Antigua, Guatemala. Today Guatemala is trying to diversify its economy,

but coffee continues to provide more than half the export revenue.

9

Treating Economic Instability

S HE does not know it, but the American house-wife frequently is Topic A in Central America. It is neither her charm nor her beauty that preoccupies Central Americans; it is her market basket. She is the biggest consumer of just about everything Central America exports: coffee, bananas, sugar. Whether she buys, what she buys and how much she pays determine, in large measure, the health of the Central American economy. If the price of coffee at her supermarket goes up five or 10 cents a pound, the economy of every Central American country that produces coffee prospers. The *finca* owners prosper most of all, of course, but the middle classes do, too, and the workers on the *fincas* prosper in a way: they have work. If the price of coffee tumbles, the misery spreads through every economic level.

The situation can be understood more clearly by examining Costa Rica. As elsewhere in Central America, much of the land is concentrated in just a few hands. But Costa Rica, as we have noted, also has a sizable class of small farmholders who own enough land to produce crops for cash, not patches just large

133

enough to produce maize for their families. About 20 per cent of Costa Rica's farms are 50 manzanas (86 acres) or more in size, and these farms occupy 81 per cent of the country's cultivated land. There are enough small farmers to make them important to Costa Rica's economy.

Most of them grow coffee. Costa Rica was the first nation in Central America to grow coffee. It started doing so back in 1796, and coffee has been a major export crop since the early 1830s. Let the price of coffee drop and the result is almost instantly visible. The small farmers stop making purchases and the economy simply comes apart.

This connection between the price the American housewife pays for what she buys at her supermarket and the state of the Central American economy has become an obsession with many Central Americans (as, indeed, it has with Latin Americans in general). Central Americans are convinced that if the housewife could only be persuaded—or forced—to pay 10 cents more for a pound of coffee, or three cents more for a pound of bananas, or five cents more for a pound of cocoa, Central America would be able to emerge from poverty.

Once a visitor to San José suggested to former President José Figueres that perhaps the Alliance for Progress (see Chapter 6) might do something to help Central America solve its economic problems. Figueres exploded. "We're bleeding to death," he said, "and you offer us a court plaster." At that moment the price of coffee was barely high enough to meet the cost of production, and Costa Rica (like every other coffee producer in Latin America) was being hurt. What Figueres was attempting to make clear was that the United States could do more to revive the Central American economy by raising the price of coffee than it could by infusing the area with Alliance money.

THIS attitude is not confined to Central America; its most eloquent spokesman, in fact, is Dr. Raúl Prebisch, an Argentine economist. Agriculture is, of course, the basis of the Latin American economy, and agricultural prices fluctuate wildly. In 1960, for example, the average price of bananas fell to 3.8 cents a pound; in 1961 the price rose to six cents. Similarly, in 1962 the average world price of sugar was 2.9 cents; by 1963 the world price had risen to 8.5 cents.

Such price fluctuations naturally make Latin America's economy basically unstable; even worse, Dr. Prebisch says, there has been a tendency over the long run for the price of imported manufactured goods to rise in relation to agricultural export prices. This, of course, causes a deficit in the trade balance of the exporting agricultural country and a resulting drain on its finances. Dr. Prebisch argues that "the declining terms of trade," as this relationship is called, increasingly worsen for Latin America. In theory, the price of manufactured goods should fall as industrial manufacturers increase productive efficiency. In recent years this has been taking place, but the prices of agricultural commodities have been falling at a faster rate.

MANY U.S. economists do not accept Dr. Prebisch's proposed solutions to the problem of the declining terms of trade. To put it simply, Dr. Prebisch proposes to build industry in the agricultural nations, shift labor from agriculture to manufacturing, and arrange for the raising and stabilizing of the prices paid for agricultural commodities by industrialized nations. Most Central Americans, however, do accept Dr. Prebisch's solutions. They are convinced that the U.S. and other industrialized nations should, above all, agree to raise the prices they pay for imported agricultural products.

Although the U.S., which drinks half of the coffee brewed in the world, agreed in 1963 to sign an international agreement to control the marketing of coffee, it has in general resisted pressure to attempt to fix prices. Many U.S. economists have argued that price-fixing can work only in the short run; in the long run, they insist, price-fixing must lead to increased production, which sooner or later would destroy the whole price-fixing structure. There is, moreover, a further argument against price-fixing. Without social reform leading to a more equitable distribution of land and wealth, the principal beneficiary of higher prices in Central America would be the oligarchy, not the agricultural workers.

There is certainly ample evidence, from U.S. experience, to suggest that price-fixing creates as many problems as it solves. Perhaps the international coffee agreement will work, because the signatories include consumers as well as producers. However, even many Central Americans are keeping their fingers crossed, for obviously Central America is not the only place in the world where coffee can be grown, and there are always loopholes in laws. Ethiopia, for example, today supplies 2 per cent of the world's coffee, and thus is by no means a formidable competitor on the international market. Nor has Ethiopia committed itself to sign the coffee agreement. Says a Guatemalan coffee grower: "I recently was in Ethiopia. Coffee grows wild there. You just have to pick it. Sooner or later, Ethiopia—or somebody else—is bound to make the agreement unworkable."

The fact is that price-fixing would not solve Central America's economic problems, even if it could be made to work. Because of the population explosion, the Central American nations must expand their gross national products by 3.5 per cent a year just to stay in the same place. Central America cannot possibly achieve this rate of expansion by producing more and more of what it produces now. There is a limit to the amount of coffee the world can drink; right now, consumption of coffee is rising at the rate of 3 per cent a year, and it is unlikely that advertising campaigns could make it rise significantly faster. Per capita consumption of bananas is relatively static in the U.S., the world's largest importer of the fruit. At best, pegging the price of the products Central America produces for export could be only a palliative.

IN the long run, Central America may be able to exploit some of its natural resources as a source of revenue. Guatemala has iron ore and timber. El Salvador has forests of mahogany. Honduras has copper, lead, zinc, iron and coal. Costa Rica has quartz, mercury, sulphur, granite, oil and copper. But only recently have the capital and the skills required to exploit such resources begun to be available in the region. For the time being and for the foreseeable future, Central America's primary resource will remain the land itself.

Unfortunately, Central America does not fully exploit that resource. In Nicaragua, three million acres could be cultivated; only one million acres are presently being farmed or put to pasturage. An estimated 90 per cent of the good flatland in Honduras lies fallow; the most intensely cultivated land in the country consists of small and relatively unproductive hillside plots. In Guatemala, large areas of the tropical plains are underutilized. Only El Salvador exploits its land to the fullest: almost three fifths of the country is in farms or pasturage.

ONE reason for the underuse of the land has been the failure of the Central American Governments to build roads. Roads are now being built at a rapid pace, but much of Honduras remains unpopulated because it is inaccessible. Until recently, the Petén region of Guatemala was equally inaccessible. Coastal regions of Panama are almost uninhabited because of the lack of roads.

The cultivated land is, moreover, badly distributed in several of the countries. In El Salvador, 2.5 per cent of the farms cover 60 per cent of the agricultural land; in Guatemala, three tenths of 1 per cent of the farms encompass 50 per cent of the farmland.

These *latifundios*, or great landholdings, usually are relatively efficient producers. Their owners, however, do not fully utilize all the land available on their estates, and much of it constitutes some of the best and most accessible acreage in Central America. By and large, the owners grow only crops they can export for dollars, not basic foods for local consumption.

Having sold the crops abroad, they have generally kept the revenues abroad. A Salvadoran economist recently estimated that in some years as much as six sevenths of the money Salvadoran coffee plantations received for coffee shipped to New York remained in New York. Admittedly, these were years of political turmoil in El Salvador: the Catorce Grande usually reinvest their money in their own country, and in 1961, in an effort to halt the flight of capital abroad, Salvadoran exporters were required by law to deposit their dollar profits in El Salvador's Central Reserve Bank. However, since political turmoil is almost a way of life in Central America, banking money abroad is a common practice in the area.

Understandably, the oligarchy uses its economic power to perpetuate that power. While Central America is today pushing the construction of a broad transportation network, the roads of Central America were originally built to link the ports with the great estates. The Central American tax system was also designed for the benefit of the landowners. The Governments derive their revenues primarily from duties on imports and from excise taxes. The burden of the income tax falls on the middle class. The real wealth of every Central American nation, as we have seen, lies in the land, and the oligarchy everywhere has made certain that land taxes are light.

Even more important, the *latifundios* have brought about the creation of *minifundios,* or minutely small holdings. Since the overwhelming majority of Central Americans live on the land, and since most of the land is owned by only a few families, most Central American farms are large enough only to grow sufficient maize for one family. Agriculturally, El Salvador is the most highly developed nation in Central America. Yet even in El Salvador, 80 per cent of the farms are less than 13 acres in size; in Costa Rica and Nicaragua any holding smaller than 85 acres is considered a subsistence farm, capable of producing only enough to meet the minimal needs of a single family, and some 75 per cent of the farms in those two countries are less than that size.

Subsistence farmers do almost nothing to sustain the economy. They can buy very little because they rarely have cash. Moreover, since the subsistence farmers have very little food to ship to market, food in the cities is sometimes scarce.

In some cases, the Central American republics actually must import foodstuffs. El Salvador has the highest population density in Central America, and its food needs are therefore greater than those of the rest of the republics. Yet, while nearly 60 per cent of El Salvador's economically active population is engaged in agriculture, and the country is one of the most efficient producers in the region, El Salvador must regularly import maize and other foodstuffs.

If all the Central American republics were like Costa Rica, with its relatively substantial class of small farm owners, the population as a whole obviously would be far more prosperous. Costa Rica's per capita income is not so high as Panama's, and it is only $100 or so higher than the per capita incomes of the other Central American countries. But a recent survey reported that in the Central American Common Market, Costa Rica was, per capita, far ahead of its sister republics in the registration of automotive vehicles; in the number of telephones in use; in the circulation of daily newspapers; and in the import of sewing machines, structural steel, flat glass, refrigerators, watches and gasoline.

The overwhelming number of the people of Central America derive their livings from the land—in El Salvador, 60 per cent of the working population; in Honduras, 84 per cent; in Guatemala and Nicaragua, 68 per cent. In Costa Rica, 45 per cent of the working population is engaged in pursuits other than agriculture—in service occupations, in trade, in construction, in transport and in manufacturing. Such opportunities for employment exist in part because of the economic activity generated by the small farmers producing crops for cash.

Over the years the maldistribution of the land in Central America—*latifundios* on the one hand, *minifundios* on the other—has caused leftists in Central America and liberals in the United States to clamor for "land reform." They want the great estates taken over by the Governments of Central America and broken up into small farms for redistribution to the landless. Some critics point to Costa Rica's relative prosperity, stability, literacy and democracy as indicative of what could be accomplished by abolishing the system of *latifundios* and *minifundios* in favor of a system of small holdings.

The argument is based on a misconception. Actually, Costa Rica does have *minifundios* and *latifundios:* three tenths of 1 per cent of the farms cover 35

FLYING THE FLAG OF CONVENIENCE

A source of income for two Central American countries—Panama and Honduras—is the granting of permission to U.S. shipowners to register vessels under their flags. Panama received some two million dollars from U.S. owners in 1963, Honduras $51,000. For the shipowners, the practice is also advantageous. Their tax rates on such vessels are lower than on U.S.-registered ships, and they may pay crewmen of other than U.S. nationality the wage rates of their own countries, which average 70 to 80 per cent less than American union scales. The practice —known as flying the "flag of convenience" or the "flag of necessity"—became widespread early in World War II when the U.S. Neutrality Act forbade the shipping of goods to belligerents in American bottoms. Today some 450 vessels, one half of the active U.S. Merchant Marine, fly foreign flags.

per cent of the land. And although Costa Rica has been called "the Switzerland of Central America," it has innumerable economic problems. These include not only the fluctuation in prices of Costa Rica's major exports but also the population growth rate, which at 4 per cent a year is one of the greatest in the world. The small farms cannot even begin to cope with the problems created by this population growth because their capacities for increasing production are limited by the extent to which they can use machinery and in the capital they have available for weed killers, fertilizers and the like.

Some *latifundios* are inefficient, but that is primarily because of the attitudes of the men who own and run them. Actually, many types of farming cannot be conducted efficiently except on big estates. U.S. agriculture is the most efficient in the world, and in the U.S. the size of the average farm is constantly on the increase.

There is, of course, no reason why the unused land in Central America should not be placed under cultivation. Guatemala is endeavoring to bring more land into production by taxing unused farmland at a rate which increases with the number of years the land has been left idle. Beyond that, however, there is the larger problem of opening up the interior. It takes money to build roads into the interior; it takes additional funds to clear opened land; in some cases the land must be irrigated, and that is expensive, too.

MOREOVER, settlers cannot simply be dumped on new land. They must have homes, fertilizer, machinery and food to live on until they can bring in a crop. They require schools and clinics. The poorer Central Americans could not provide such things themselves because they are almost penniless. In Honduras, three quarters of the farmers have never been able to afford even a plow. Most of them live in mud huts on dirt floors.

Nor is money the only problem. A vast program of education is needed, too, for the fact is that most subsistence farmers do not really know how to farm. Even if they could afford plows, they would not be able to use them properly.

Central America's economic problems are clearly formidable, yet they are not insuperable. Under the Alliance for Progress, there is money available for roads and homes, schools and clinics. Nor is Central America without capital itself. The trouble is that the Central American Governments are unable—or unwilling—to collect taxes.

One answer to Central America's problems would be a tax system that would provide money for economic development. Another would be social and welfare legislation. Obviously, wages could not be pushed too high without crippling production. However, the 60-cents-a-day minimum wage and 10-cents-a-day food allowance now required by law in El Salvador could hardly be called an unconscionable burden on the Catorce Grande. Similarly, welfare funds could not be pushed too high without creating government deficits and inflation, but an equitable tax system would enable Central America to spend more on welfare than it does now.

DIVERSIFICATION of agriculture would certainly help the Central American economy. If the big landowners were to produce a great variety of crops, they would have fewer worries about fluctuations in world prices. There would be fewer complaints like that voiced a few years ago by Ricardo Castro Beeche, the distinguished editor of *La Nación* of Costa Rica. "What difference would it make," he asked, "if the householders of the United States were to pay ten cents . . . more for a pound of coffee?"

Along with diversification of agriculture must come industrialization. At present, Central America needs every dollar agricultural exports bring to buy manufactured goods abroad. The region is not, to state the obvious, on the verge of becoming a great industrial complex. It will continue to import trucks and tractors and heavy machinery. Nevertheless, there are a great many articles Central America now imports that it could make for itself. Even limited industrialization would provide work for the jobless in the cities and for those constantly being dispossessed from the land by the population explosion.

The American housewife cannot solve Central America's problems for it, no matter how much she pays at her supermarket for coffee. There is no reason, however, why Central America should not be able to solve most of its own problems. The question is: will it?

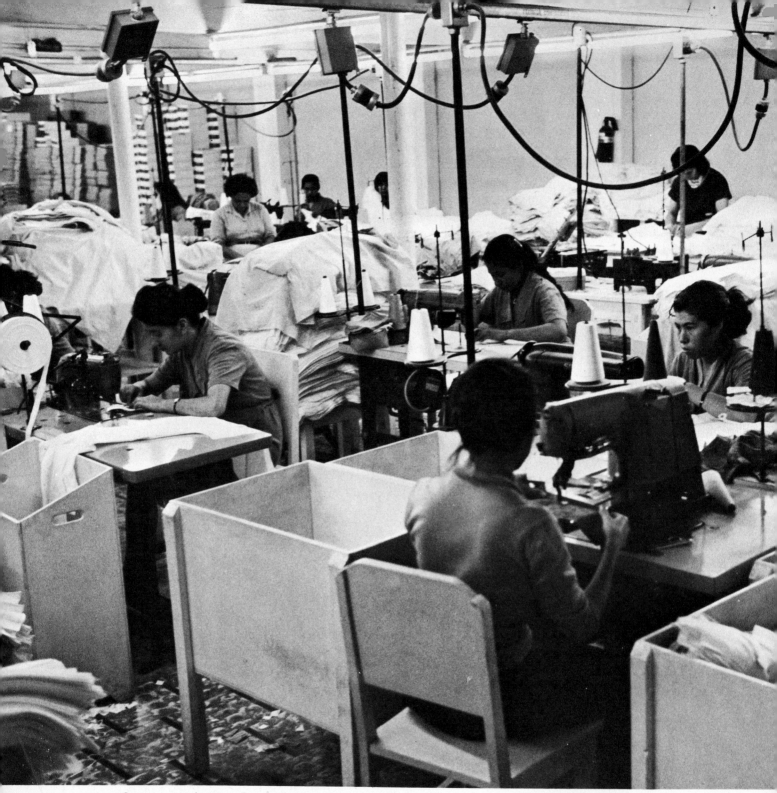

Seamstresses in the Arrow factory in Guatemala City turn out 9,000 shirts a month for sale in the Central American Common Market area.

Benefits Derived from a Common Market

A Central American Common Market was first proposed in 1950 to create a single free-trade area with a profit potential great enough to make industrializing feasible. Trade arrangements among the five member nations—Nicaragua, El Salvador, Honduras, Costa

SHOE LASTS await the next production step in a San Salvador plant. The country's largest shoe factory, it makes 4,700 shoes each day for both internal and export sale in Central America.

UNCURED TIRES hang on racks (*below*) in the Ginsa tire factory in Guatemala. Ginsa was granted a five-year tire-production monopoly in the Market area to assure it sufficient sales.

The factory employs 75 workers, who earn about $15 a week each.

Rica and Guatemala—are not yet fully worked out, but since 1960, when the Market really got started, internal trade has grown by some 30 per cent. Outside capital is being attracted, and new factories are being built. Perhaps best, wages are slowly rising.

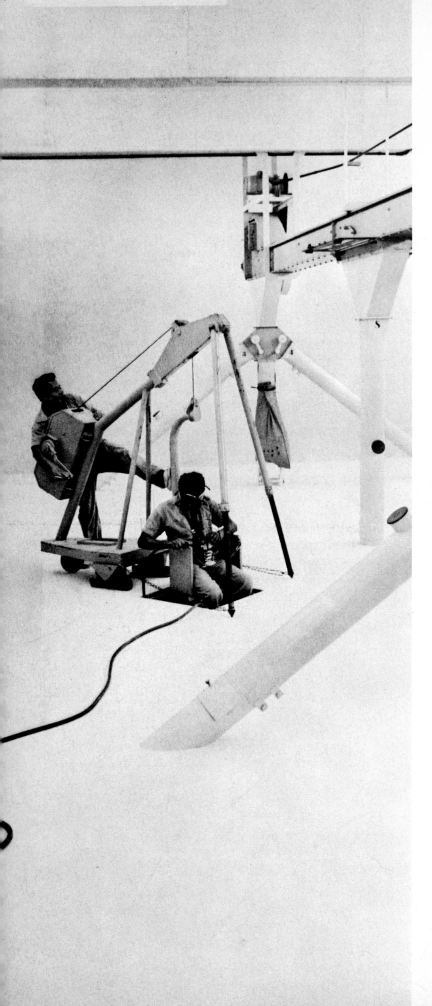

NEW INDUSTRIES are being started by investors drawn to the inducements offered by the Common Market

MILES OF YARN are wound on spools *(above)* in a San Salvador textile plant. Ninety per cent Japanese-owned, it exports 65 per cent of its yarn to other Central American countries.

INTERIOR OF A SILO in a San Salvador mill *(left)* is cleaned for flour storage. Now owned entirely by local businessmen, the mill was started with the help of the Pillsbury Company.

ELECTRIC POWER, symbolized in a mural *(opposite)*, is generated by a Japanese-made turbine in El Salvador. The plant is Government-owned, but private companies distribute the power.

PORT FACILITIES at Acajutla, El Salvador, are dominated by a soaring observation tower at the left for the use of officials and a mile-long pier built in 1961. The port is expected to serve as the Common Market's principal outlet on the Pacific Ocean.

SWEEPING VIEW is afforded from a terrace *(right)* of the Cerro Verde Mountain Hotel in El Salvador. Jutting out at left is the overhanging roof of another part of the hotel, which was constructed by the Government in 1958 to attract foreign tourists.

CIVIC CENTER in Guatemala City *(below)* includes the Municipal Building *(background),* constructed in 1956 for the use of city officials, and the Social Security Building, adorned with a mosaic designed by the Guatemalan-born artist Carlos Mérida.

SLEEK BUILDINGS *rise as the economic pace of the area begins to quicken*

10

Toward Tomorrow

THE history of Central America is a history of broken dreams. Yet today Central America has reason for hope. And for once, reality appears to justify rhetoric.

The reality is the Central American Common Market, established by Guatemala, El Salvador, Nicaragua, Honduras and Costa Rica in a series of treaties signed between 1951 and 1962. Someday Panama, too, may join. The Panamanians are divided on the question of entering the Market because the Canal dominates the country's economy. Direct payments from the United States for the right to maintain the Canal, wages paid to Panamanians, and U.S. buying in Panama provide one fifth of Panama's gross national income. The influx of U.S. dollars has made wages and prices in Panama higher than elsewhere in Central America; those Panamanians who maintain that Panama should remain aloof from the Common Market argue that it could not compete with such relatively low-cost producers as Guatemala and El Salvador.

Taken by itself, the argument may appear convincing; still, the odds are that Panama will eventually decide to join the Common Market. The reason is simple: even in its short life the Market has proved a considerable success.

The basis of Central America's Common Market plan is, of course, the gradual lowering and eventual elimination of tariffs between the member nations. In a year or two, according to present timetables, tariffs will have disappeared as far as trade within the area is concerned; protective tariffs on goods coming from outside the Market region will have been made uniform.

That is only part of the plan, however. Trade cannot flow without transportation; Central America is therefore creating a coordinated highway system. Industry cannot develop without credit; in 1961, for that reason, the Common Market nations created a Central American Bank for Economic Integration to finance new industries. Factories need power; the Common Market nations will be well on the way toward an integrated electric-power grid by 1970. Trade is also facilitated by easily convertible currency; a Central American Clearing House was established in 1961.

ONE of the principal reasons industry never developed in Central America is that no Central American nation is big enough to provide a market for any sizable industry. Costa Rica, with a population of 1.3 million, certainly is not of sufficient size; nor Nicaragua, with a population of 1.6 million; nor even Guatemala, with 4.1 million.

Together, however, the five nations in the Central American Market do provide a significant market— 12 million people, with a combined gross national product of more than $2.5 billion.

Another aspect of the over-all Central American development plan, therefore, is the encouragement of "integrated" industrial enterprises which need a market at least as large as the five Central American countries combined in order to operate with reasonable efficiency and profit. Generous tax and tariff concessions granted such enterprises would give them virtual monopolies of their fields within the Market. Each of the Market countries is scheduled to have at least one protected industry. Considerable controversy, however, has developed over the "integrated" plan, and there is a trend toward its modification. In its stead might come a system whereby any company could qualify for a protective tariff as soon as its output grew large enough to cover more than half of the needs of the Market area. No company would be granted a monopoly.

There are other obstacles to industrialization in Central America. In addition to rugged terrain and a poor but improving transportation network, the area has, as we have noted, a limited store of industrial raw materials and a largely illiterate population that subsists on incomes barely sufficient to pay for food and shelter. For these people there is no money available to buy manufactured goods.

But steps toward solving these problems are being taken. One important stimulus in the development of the Central American Common Market has been the Alliance for Progress. Under the Alliance's provisions, the United States is now allocating some $80 million a year to the Common Market countries. Not all of the money is being expended wisely or well, but the aid has certainly been a significant factor in the Market's success. Much of the money has been spent to finance private industry.

One of the best ways to judge the region's recent economic progress is simply to walk into the leading hotel of any Central American capital. The visitor will find it bustling with U.S. and European businessmen carrying dispatch cases filled with plans for investing in Central America. Nor do these plans exist merely on paper. In El Salvador, for example, Phelps Dodge of the U.S. has built a two-million-dollar copper wire and cable plant; Unilever of London and Rotterdam has joined forces with the De Sola family of El Salvador to set up a company for the manufacture of soap, margarine, toothpaste and dehydrated soup. Philips of the Netherlands has built an appliance and light-bulb plant.

WHAT is true of El Salvador is true almost everywhere. Allied Chemical is building a refinery in Costa Rica in partnership with Costa Rican businessmen and the Costa Rican Government. Hercules Powder, Pennsalt Chemicals and Nicaragua's Institute for National Development are planning to build a caustic soda and chlorine plant and an insecticide plant in Nicaragua, a project that has been granted integrated status by the Common Market. Guatemala has a number of new plants, including the Ginsa tire factory, the other of the two integrated enterprises so far authorized.

Industrialization has begun to change the face of Central America in other ways. A new cement plant went into production in Costa Rica in April 1964. Industria Nacional de Cemento, S.A., is Costa Rica's first cement plant; by removing the need for cement imports it will save the country $1.4 million a year in foreign exchange. Perhaps even more important, it was in large part financed by the sale of stock to more than 3,000 ordinary persons—shoemakers, waiters, bartenders, students, newspaper reporters, secretaries and barbers. To make it possible for such people to purchase the shares (at $15 each), the company sold them on the installment plan: $4.50 down, with the balance in 24 monthly payments.

IN Central America, such a stock-flotation scheme was revolutionary. Even in Costa Rica, there had never before been a widely held corporation. If Cemento, S.A., is profitable, the idea of starting companies through stock issues will no doubt spread. And this not only should lead to greater economic development; it also should add a stabilizing factor to Central American politics. People who own stock are not very likely to riot in the streets.

The impact of recent industrial expansion is being felt even in the countryside. Costa Rica, for example, has been troubled by a shortage of electric power brought about not only by its rapid population increase but by increased industrialization itself. Under a project of the Inter-American Development Bank, an agency that supplies funds for economic and social programs with capital supplied by the U.S. and Latin American countries, the country set about rehabilitating and extending its electric-power distribution system. This has brought electricity to a number of rural areas that never had it before.

One of them is Puente de Piedra, about 25 miles northwest of San José. Puente de Piedra is a moderately prosperous community of small sugar planters and coffee growers. When they heard the power line was coming, they wired their homes and bought whatever electrical appliances they could—radios, electric irons, electric stoves. Some of the more prosperous farmers even bought TV sets. Soon, teachers noticed a rise in the marks their students were scoring on tests. With electric light, the children could study at night. There was also a rise in political discussion in the community, because the farmers had become more conversant with national and world events by listening to news broadcasts.

The effect of aid programs largely financed by the U.S. is equally visible. When the U.S. cut off trade with Cuba in 1962 after the breakdown in American-Cuban relations, American cigar smokers were dismayed; most tobacco leaf does not compare with Cuban tobacco. Fortunately, a Cuban tobacco grower managed to spirit out 12 pounds of Cuban seed as he went into exile. Inter-American Development Bank officials saw an opportunity to end the agony of the American cigar smokers and, at the same time, give Honduras a new export crop. They sent a team of Cuban exiles to Honduras with the seed to show Honduran farmers how to grow tobacco—how to plow the soil deeply, irrigate gently without flooding, and build curing sheds.

Ordinarily, the Hondurans might have paid their peasants 50 or 70 cents a day. Under prodding from the aid officials and from the Cubans, they agreed to pay $1.25 and even $1.50. The effect on the surrounding towns was dramatic. For it was not only the local cafés that got the workers' pay; the shopkeepers did, too. Suddenly, there were buyers for radios, bicycles, sewing machines and clothing.

SO there is indeed reason for hope in Central America. Nevertheless, the region has its pessimists, who cannot look into the future without remembering the past. They fear the past may blight the future—and their fear is justified. For industrialization and economic development are not panaceas. The wealth they create does not always trickle down. On the contrary, the changes generated by industrialization can intensify poverty and misery.

The United States has, of course, seen such phenomena in recent years. Technological advance created a boom; it also created an increasing number of unemployed and unemployables. Such a process could take place even more easily in Central America, because the rate of illiteracy there is higher and the proportion of unskilled persons is greater.

One of Central America's major political and social problems is the growth of the city slums. Irrigation and the electrification of Central America's farms and the construction of fertilizer plants will, of course, increase production and reduce costs on the farms; at the same time, however, they may aggravate the slum problem by lessening the need for workers in the fields. The workers will have no place to go but to the cities. There, like the present slum dwellers, driven into the cities by the population explosion, they will find themselves—because they have no skills—unable to get jobs in the humming new factories, offices and shops.

An increase in the number of oases of prosperity in Central America's generally barren economic desert could only aggravate social tension. The rise of a prosperous middle class and a skilled working class drawing good wages inevitably will raise prices. At the same time, such a development will constantly remind slum dwellers of their misery.

OBVIOUSLY, prosperity for some cannot be enough. Prosperity must be shared. Unfortunately, those who rule Central America are often too busy attempting to modernize and industrialize to worry much about the problems that modernization and industrialization will eventually create. And many of the Central American leaders actively oppose doing anything toward solving them.

One great need of Central America, for example, is education. The displaced peasants can be made employable only if they first learn to read and write. However, schools and teachers cost money, and that means higher taxes—and of course taxes are easy to propose, but difficult to impose.

The simple fact is this: industrialization could very well aggravate political tensions, unless there is social and economic reform. Without it, the slums will become an ever more fertile breeding ground for Castroism. Let one Central American country go Castroite and economic progress will come to a halt. Money will flee into the New York Stock Exchange and U.S. and Swiss banks; the U.S. and European businessmen with the bulging dispatch cases will catch the first plane home.

There is a growing tendency in the United States to applaud when the military seizes control of a Latin American government to "prevent a Communist take-over." At times this reaction is justified. The threat of Communism frequently is real. Moreover, military leaders are not always reactionary; they are not always tyrannical and rapacious. Sometimes,

however, they are. They work hand in glove with the oligarchs, suppressing the industrial workers and the farm workers in return for a license to enrich themselves. A military take-over of this sort, therefore, may open the way to a Communist revolution by intensifying the grievances of the lower classes instead of alleviating them.

The stability of Central America is threatened by another problem, that of a continuing tradition of meddling in other countries' affairs.

Nicaragua, Honduras and the Dominican Republic all gave military aid to Costa Rican Government forces during the Costa Rican civil war in 1948, while Guatemala supported rebel forces. Such clashes are by no means unusual. As recently as 1959, Costa Rica permitted a group of Nicaraguan rebels to use its territory as a launching base for an invasion of Nicaragua. In more recent years, the borders have been quiet, but since the enmities remain, the danger of further clashes cannot be ruled out.

THE outlook is not all bright; it is not all black. Nevertheless, the reasons for hope outweigh the reasons for pessimism. Even among the oligarchs, there is a growing realization of the desirability of social and economic reform, especially among the younger men educated in the United States who are capable of understanding the difference between an income tax and Communism. At the same time, the development of a middle class and a class of skilled workers is creating a significantly large group of politically sophisticated voters.

In fact, if Castro subversion and internal political upheavals do not upset the Common Market's plans, Central America will be united economically within a decade. There are those who believe that economic unity will sooner or later lead to political unity. That, perhaps, is too wild a dream—but perhaps it is not. For diversified economic development should bring with it a substantial enlargement of a middle class whose members may well tend toward a Central American rather than a purely national outlook. And with that, Central Americans may learn that there is more than sentiment in a motto which long ago became an intrinsic part of the political thinking of their North American neighbors—"In union, there is strength."

In a Government-sponsored reading class in Guatemala, an illiterate peasant woman slowly copies a lesson from a book held by her child.

THE CHALLENGE *presented by the poverty and ignorance of centuries . . .*

A 1963 conference of the Central American Common Market is opened in Costa Rica by leaders of the five member nations, joined by

. . . shows promise of being met as Central Americans begin to work together

Panama's President Roberto F. Chiari (right foreground), who came as an observer, and U.S. President John F. Kennedy (left center).

to promote economic well-being and thus open the doors to progress and stability

Appendix

HISTORICAL DATES

c. 10,000 B.C.	Various Indian tribes arrive in Central America and slowly begin to create several distinct cultures
500 B.C.- 300 A.D.	Formative period of Maya culture: early temple cities are built and hieroglyphic writing is developed
300-900	Classic period of Maya civilization: mathematics, astronomy, architecture, religion and art all flourish
900-1400	Gradually the cities are taken over by the jungle as Maya civilization declines, probably as a result of internal dissension and invasion by Mexican tribes
1502	First Europeans, members of Columbus' fourth expedition, land in Central America. Columbus himself goes ashore at Cape Honduras
1509	First European settlement on the mainland of America is established in Panama by a Spanish expedition
1513	Spaniards in Panama, led by Vasco Núñez de Balboa, reach the Pacific coast for the first time
1524	The first Spanish women arrive in Central America. Spanish expeditions subdue natives of El Salvador and invade Guatemala. Granada and León, first permanent Spanish settlements, are established in Nicaragua
1540-1550	The refusal of many Indians to work for white men prompts the importation of Negro slaves from Africa
1544	Central America is unified politically by Spain under the Audiencia, a court with administrative and judicial functions
1570	The first Audiencia is replaced by the Audiencia de Guatemala, under whose provisions most of Central America is ruled for two and one half centuries
1697	Final Spanish conquest in Central America destroys the last stronghold of the Maya in Petén, northern Guatemala
1811	First revolt against Spanish rule erupts in El Salvador
1821	Officials of the Audiencia and some powerful landowners declare their independence from Spain and set up the United Provinces of Central America
1822-1823	Central America becomes part of the newly independent Mexican "empire," which shortly collapses
1823	Central America is again declared free by a constituent assembly, but real unity is frustrated by animosity between conservatives and liberals in the five constituent states of Central America. Panama, declaring its independence from Spain, decides to become part of Greater Colombia
1838	The powerless federal congress decrees that all the states are free to form their own governments. The Central American union breaks up
1839	Francisco Morazán of Honduras makes last attempt to unify the republics. He fails and is exiled
1839-1865	Rafael Carrera, President of Guatemala for most of this period, repeatedly attacks other republics, deposing liberal governments and establishing conservative ones
1855	An American, William Walker, invades Nicaragua with a small force and in 1856 becomes President, defeating the conservatives
1857	Forces drawn from Costa Rica, Honduras, Guatemala and El Salvador drive Walker from Nicaragua. Walker tries to reinvade Central America twice and is finally executed in 1860
1873-1885	Justo Rufino Barrios becomes President of Guatemala. Liberal and anticlerical, he becomes the rallying point for anticonservative movements throughout Central America and succeeds in putting liberal governments in power in several countries
1885	Barrios tries to unite the Central American republics forcibly and is killed in battle
1893-1909	Liberal revolt brings José Santos Zelaya to power in Nicaragua. Zelaya becomes a tyrant remarkable in an era of bloody dictatorships
1898-1920	Manuel Estrada Cabrera, another corrupt dictator, rules as President of Guatemala
1903	After the Colombian Congress rejects a proposed treaty giving the U.S. the right to dig a canal across the Isthmus of Panama, the U.S. arranges a successful Panamanian revolt against Colombia and quickly recognizes the new country's independence. A treaty is signed with Panama, giving the U.S. permission to dig the canal and control a strip of land across the Isthmus
1912	Strife between liberals and conservatives erupts in Nicaragua and the U.S. dispatches Marines to the country to "protect American citizens," a procedure repeated several times in ensuing years
1914	First ocean-going vessel passes through the Panama Canal
1931-1948	Tiburcio Carías Andino rules as dictator of Honduras. Jorge Ubico, a progressive and effective if ruthless leader, is President of Guatemala. Ubico improves the nation's communications and stimulates the economy
1936	New treaty is signed by Panama and the U.S. It releases Panama from its status as a U.S. protectorate and increases U.S. payments for its Canal rights
1937-1956	General Anastasio Somoza is President of Nicaragua
1951-1954	Jacobo Arbenz Guzmán is the dictator of Guatemala. He is overthrown by the Army after his regime shows strong Communist influence
1951-1962	The Central American republics sign a group of treaties designed "to fortify the ties that unite them." The pacts establish a Common Market in the area, providing for free trade and other forms of economic cooperation among the members. Panama is invited to join
1958-1963	Miguel Ydígoras Fuentes holds office as President of Guatemala. He is ousted by the Army to prevent the election of a leftist successor
1962	Francisco José Orlich is elected President of Costa Rica. Costa Rica joins the Common Market
1963	The Army takes over the Government of Honduras, ousting President Villeda Morales. Colonel Enrique Peralta seizes power in Guatemala
1964	Anti-American riots break out in Panama, and U.S.-Panama diplomatic relations are temporarily severed

152

FOR FURTHER READING

Chapter 1: Nations Escaping the Past

Adams, Richard N., *Cultural Surveys of Panama — Nicaragua — Guatemala — El Salvador—Honduras*. World Health Organization, Washington, D.C., 1957.

Carr, Archie F., *High Jungles and Low*. University of Florida Press, 1953.

Hanson, Earl Parker, ed., *The New World Guides to Latin American Republics*, Vol. I, 3rd ed. Duell, Sloan and Pearce, 1950.

Henry, O., *The Complete Works of O. Henry*, Vol. I, *Cabbages and Kings*. Doubleday & Company, 1953.

Jones, Chester L., *Costa Rica and Civilization in the Caribbean*. University of Wisconsin Press, 1935. *Guatemala, Past and Present*. University of Minnesota Press, 1940.

Stephens, John Lloyd, *Incidents of Travel in Central America, Chiapas, and Yucatan*. First published in 1841 by Harper; reissued by Rutgers University Press in 2 vols., 1949.

Whetten, Nathan L., *Guatemala, the Land and the People*. Yale University Press, 1961.

Wilgus, A. Curtis, ed., *The Caribbean: The Central American Area*. University of Florida Press, 1961.

Chapter 2: The Maya

Jennings, Jesse, and Norbeck, Edward, eds., *Prehistoric Man in the New World*. University of Chicago Press, 1964.

Morley, Sylvanus, *The Ancient Maya*, rev. by George W. Brainerd, 3rd ed. Stanford University Press, 1956.

Thompson, J. Eric S., *The Rise and Fall of Maya Civilization*. University of Oklahoma Press, 1954.

Chapter 3: The Spanish Conquest

Bannon, John Francis, S.J., and Dunne, Peter Masten, S.J., *Latin America, An Historical Survey*. The Bruce Publishing Company, Milwaukee, 1947.

Bourne, Edward Gaylord, *Spain in America 1450-1580*. Barnes & Noble, Inc., New York, 1962.

Conquistadores, The. First-person accounts of the conquest of Mexico. Trans. and ed. by Patricia de Fuentes; preface by Howard F. Cline. The Orion Press, Inc., New York, 1963.

Crow, John A., *The Epic of Latin America*. Doubleday & Company, 1946.

de Gómara, Francisco López, *Cortés, the Life of the Conqueror by His Secretary*, trans. and ed. by Lesley Byrd Simpson. University of California Press, 1964.

de Madariaga, Salvador, *Hernán Cortés, Conqueror of Mexico*. Henry Regnery Company, Chicago, 1955.

Elliott, J. H., *Imperial Spain 1469-1716*. St. Martin's Press, New York, 1964.

Hanke, Lewis, *Bartolomé de Las Casas, An Interpretation of His Life and Writings*. Martinus Nijhoff, The Hague, 1951.

Haring, Clarence H., *The Spanish Empire in America*. Oxford University Press, New York, 1947.

Merriman, Roger Bigelow, *The Rise of the Spanish Empire in the Old World and in the New*, Vols. I through IV. The Macmillan Company, 1936.

Morison, Samuel Eliot, *Admiral of the Ocean Sea, a Life of Christopher Columbus*, Vols. I and II. Little, Brown & Company, Boston, 1942.

Peck, Anne M., *The Pageant of Middle American History*. Longmans, Green & Company, 1947.

Schurz, William L., *This New World; The Civilization of Latin America*. E. P. Dutton & Company, Inc., 1954.

Taylor, Mack, *Impetuous Alvarado*. Tardy Publishing Company, Dallas, 1936.

Chapter 4: Century of Disorder

Herring, Hubert, *A History of Latin America*. Alfred A. Knopf, 1961.

Holleran, Mary P., *Church and State in Guatemala*. Columbia University Press, 1949.

Karnes, Thomas L., *The Failure of the Union, Central America 1824-1960*. University of North Carolina Press, 1961.

Munro, Dana Gardner, *The Latin American Republics, A History*, 3rd ed. Appleton-Century-Crofts, Inc., 1960.

Rippy, Fred J., *Latin America, A Modern History*. University of Michigan Press, 1958.

Chapter 5: The U.S. Involvement

Bemis, Samuel Flagg, *A Diplomatic History of the United States*. Henry Holt and Company, Inc., 1955.

Carr, Albert Z., *The World and William Walker*. Harper and Row, 1963.

DuVal, Miles P., Jr., *Cadiz to Cathay*. Stanford University Press, 1947.

Lane, Wheaton J., *Commodore Vanderbilt*. Alfred A. Knopf, 1942.

McCain, William D., *The United States and the Republic of Panama*. Duke University Press, 1937.

Mack, Gerstle, *The Land Divided*. Alfred A. Knopf, 1944.

May, Stacy, and Plaza, Galo, *United States Business Performance Abroad: The Case Study of the United Fruit Company in Latin America*. National Planning Association, 1958.

Schneider, Ronald M., *Communism in Guatemala: 1944-1954*. Frederick A. Praeger, 1959.

Wilson, Charles Morrow, *Empire in Green and Gold*. Henry Holt and Company, 1947.

Chapters 6 and 7: The Poor, the Wealthy

Adams, Richard N., *Cultural Surveys of Panama—Nicaragua—Guatemala—El Salvador—Honduras*. World Health Organization, Washington, D.C., 1957.

Biesanz, John and Mavis, *Costa Rican Life*. Columbia University Press, 1944. *The People of Panama*. Columbia University Press, 1955.

Kelsey, Vera, and Osborne, Lilly de Jongh, *Four Keys to Guatemala*. Funk and Wagnalls, 1961.

Osborne, Lilly de Jongh, *Four Keys to El Salvador*. Funk and Wagnalls, 1956.

Chapter 8: Democrats and Dictators

Parker, Franklin D., *The Central American Republics*. Oxford University Press, London, 1964.

Rosenthal, Mario, *Guatemala, The Story of an Emergent Latin-American Democracy*. Twayne Publishers, Inc., New York, 1962.

Chapters 9 and 10: The Economy

Adler, John H., Schlesinger, Eugene R., and Olson, Ernest C., *Public Finance and Economic Development in Guatemala*. Stanford University Press, 1952.

Bureau of Foreign Commerce, U.S. Department of Commerce, *Investment in Central America*. U.S. Government Printing Office, 1956.

Checchi, Vincent, and others, *Honduras: A Problem in Economic Development*. Twentieth Century Fund, 1959.

Gordon, Lincoln, *A New Deal for Latin America: The Alliance for Progress*. Harvard University Press, 1963.

International Bank for Reconstruction and Development, *The Economic Development of Guatemala*. Johns Hopkins Press, 1951. *The Economic Development of Nicaragua*. Johns Hopkins

Press, 1953.

Manger, William, *Pan America in Crisis: The Future of the Organization of American States.* Public Affairs Press, Washington, D.C., 1961.

Martz, John D., *Central America, the Crisis and the Challenge.* University of North Carolina Press, 1959.

May, Stacy, and others, *Costa Rica: A Study in Economic Development.* Twentieth Century Fund, 1952.

Pincus, Joseph, *The Central American Common Market.* U.S. Department of State, Agency for International Development, 1962.

Radler, Don H., *El Gringo: The Yankee Image in Latin America.* Chilton, 1962.

Wallich, Henry C., Adler, John H., and others, *Public Finance in a Developing Country: El Salvador, a Case Study.* Harvard University Press, 1951.

Wilgus, A. Curtis, ed., *The Caribbean: The Central American Area.* University of Florida Press, 1961.

Withers, William, *The Economic Crisis in Latin America.* Collier—Macmillan, The Free Press of Glencoe, New York, 1964.

MAJOR POLITICAL UNITS OF CENTRAL AMERICA

PLACE	POP.	AREA	HISTORY	POLITICAL STATUS
COSTA RICA	1,333,000	19,653 sq. mi.	First Spanish settlement 1523. Became independent of Spain in 1821. Joined the Central American Federation in 1823 and has been independent since the Federation began to break up in 1838	Republic
EL SALVADOR	2,666,000	8,160 sq. mi.	First Spanish settlement 1523. Joined the Central American Federation in 1823; became independent in 1841	Republic
GUATEMALA	4,100,000	42,040 sq. mi.	First Spanish settlement 1524. Joined the Federation in 1823 and left it in 1839	Republic
HONDURAS	2,087,000	43,280 sq. mi.	First Spanish settlement 1502. Independent since it left the Central American Federation in 1838	Republic
NICARAGUA	1,630,000	57,150 sq. mi.	First Spanish settlement 1523. Broke away from the Central American Federation to become independent in 1838	Republic
PANAMA	1,160,000	28,576 sq. mi. (excl. Canal Zone)	First Spanish settlement 1503. Declared its independence from Spain in 1821 and became a part of the Republic of Colombia. Broke away from Colombian rule in 1903 and has been independent since	Republic
BRITISH HONDURAS	90,019	8,866 sq. mi.	First settlements made by British woodcutters about 1638	British colony
PANAMA CANAL ZONE	42,122	648 sq. mi.	Leased to the U.S. in 1903	U.S.-administered, but technically Panamanian, territory

CAPITAL ✓	MAJOR SOURCES OF INCOME ✓	RELIGION ✓	LANGUAGE ✓
San José	Coffee, bananas	Roman Catholic	Spanish
San Salvador	Coffee	Roman Catholic	Spanish
Guatemala City	Coffee, bananas, chicle	Roman Catholic	Spanish
Tegucigalpa	Bananas, coffee, cotton, cattle	Roman Catholic, some Protestant communities	Spanish
Managua	Bananas, cotton, coffee, sugar cane	Roman Catholic, some Protestant communities	Spanish
Panama City	Bananas, shipping	Roman Catholic, some Protestant communities	Spanish
Belize	Citrus fruits, lumber, fishing, sugar	Roman Catholic, some Protestant communities	Spanish, English
Balboa (administrative headquarters)	Canal tolls	Protestant, Roman Catholic, Jewish	English

Credits

The sources for the illustrations in this book appear below. Credits for pictures from left to right are separated by commas, from top to bottom by dashes.

Cover—Howard Sochurek
8—Howard Sochurek
15 through 24—Howard Sochurek
27—Map by Rafael Palacios
31, 32—Fritz Goro
33 through 37—Howard Sochurek
38—Fritz Goro
39, 40—Howard Sochurek
42, 43—Map by Enrico Arno
47 through 50—Howard Sochurek
51—Foto Vicente
52, 53—Howard Sochurek
54, 55—George Silk
57—The Bettmann Archive except center Culver Pictures
61—Foto Muñoz
62—Panama Canal Photo—The Bettmann Archive
63—Brown Brothers—Panama Canal Photo
64, 65—Defense Department Photos except bottom center The Bettmann Archive
66, 67—Raul Gonzalez—Dirck Halstead, George Silk, Dirck Halstead—United Press International
68, 69—Wide World—Henry Wal-lace—Raul Gonzalez, Andrew St. George
70, 71—Peter Anderson from Black Star
73, 74—The Bettmann Archive
77—Drawing by Rafael Palacios
80 through 83—Howard Sochurek
84, 85—Howard Sochurek except left John Dominis
86 through 88—Howard Sochurek
94 through 102—Howard Sochurek
110 through 117—Howard Sochurek
124, 125—George Silk, Bruce Henderson—Howard Sochurek, Cornell Capa from Magnum
126—Peter Anderson
127—Howard Sochurek except left Don Uhrbrock
128, 129—Howard Sochurek
130, 131—Michael Rougier except right Bill Eppridge
132, 133—Howard Sochurek
138, 139—Howard Sochurek except bottom right John Dominis
140 through 144—Howard Sochurek
149—Raul Gonzalez
150, 151—John Dominis

ACKNOWLEDGMENTS

The editors express their appreciation to the following scholars, who read and commented on portions of the text: William R. Coe, University Museum, University of Pennsylvania; Lewis Hanke, Professor of Latin American History, Columbia University; and Ronald Schneider, Visiting Associate Professor of Government, Columbia University.

Index

This symbol in front of a page number indicates a photograph or painting of the subject mentioned.

XX

Production staff for Time Incorporated
John L. Hallenbeck (Vice President and Director of Production)
Robert E. Foy, Caroline Ferri and Robert E. Fraser
Text photocomposed under the direction of
Albert J. Dunn and Arthur J. Dunn